BIBLE
QUIZ
SHOW

AN A-TO-Z TRIVIA CHALLENGE

BIBLE QUIZ SHOW

PAUL KENT

BARBOUR BOOKS
An Imprint of Barbour Publishing, Inc.

© 2004 by Barbour Publishing, Inc.

Previously released under the title *A to Z Bible Trivia: The Ultimate Scripture Quiz*.

ISBN 978-1-64352-466-5

All rights reserved. No part of this publication may be reproduced or transmitted for commercial purposes, except for brief quotations in printed reviews, without written permission of the publisher.

Churches and other noncommercial interests may reproduce portions of this book without the express written permission of Barbour Publishing, provided that the text does not exceed 500 words and that the text is not material quoted from another publisher. When reproducing text from this book, include the following credit line: "From *Bible Quiz Show*, published by Barbour Publishing, Inc. Used by permission."

All scripture quotations, unless otherwise indicated, are taken from the Holy Bible, New International Version®. niv®. Copyright © 1973, 1978, 1984, 2011 by Biblica, Inc.™ Used by permission. All rights reserved worldwide.

Scripture quotations marked kjv are taken from the King James Version.

Published by Barbour Books, an imprint of Barbour Publishing, Inc., 1810 Barbour Drive, Uhrichsville, Ohio 44683, www.barbourbooks.com

Our mission is to inspire the world with the life-changing message of the Bible.

Member of the
Evangelical Christian
Publishers Association

Printed in the United States of America.

CONTENTS

INTRODUCTION

You stand impatiently backstage, waiting for the announcer to call your name. Sweat beads on your brow, as much from the bright, hot lights as from your nervousness. You're the next contestant on the hit television game show, *Bible Quiz Show!*

And now, welcome. . . The voice trails off in your head as you hear your own name spoken. You walk, as if in a dream, past TV cameras and the studio audience. Will your knowledge of the Bible dazzle this crowd enough to turn their polite applause into a hearty ovation?

Now the host of the show speaks:

> *You know how our game is played—we'll ask you questions from the Bible, and you answer them. Simple enough, right? We shall see. . . .*
>
> *There are four quizzes for every letter of the alphabet—even for Q and X! Each quiz features five questions, ranging in value from 100 to 500 points—and the questions get harder as the points increase. When you've been through all four quizzes for a particular letter of the alphabet, you'll have the opportunity to Risk It!—to chance any or all of your points for that letter on one final question. You*

could potentially double your score!

We'll keep a running tally of your score, and by the end of the show, we'll know whether you belong in the Bible Hall of Fame. . .or the Hall of Shame. Are you ready to begin?

You croak a weak "yes" and make your way to the contestant's chair. Flashing signs prompt the audience to applaud as you await the first question. . . .

NOTE: The New International Version is the primary translation used in this book. Where wording differs between the NIV and the King James Version, both are listed—NIV first, KJV second.

ABEL

Are you "able" to handle "Abel"? Most everyone knows Abel was the world's first murder victim. . .but what else do you know about this unfortunate man?

Answers on next page.

100
What "first couple" gave birth to Abel?

200
What unaccepted offering provoked Cain's murder of Abel?

300
What five-word question did Cain use to dismiss God's question about Abel's whereabouts?

400
What part of Abel did God tell Cain "cries out to me from the ground"?

500
What third son did Eve say God gave her in place of the murdered Abel?

ABEL ANSWERS

100
Adam and Eve (Genesis 4:1–2)

200
fruits of the soil (Genesis 4:3–5)

300
"Am I my brother's keeper?" (Genesis 4:9)

400
his blood (Genesis 4:10)

500
Seth (Genesis 4:25)

Your Score for This Quiz:
_____Points

AKA

You've seen these initials in TV police shows—they stand for "also known as." What do you know about the alternative names of Bible characters?

Answers on next page.

100
What apostle and New Testament author was originally known as Saul?

200
What fisherman turned apostle was also known as Simon or Cephas?

300
What Old Testament prophet once had his name changed to "Belteshazzar"?

400
What nickname, meaning "Son of Encouragement," did the apostles give to Joseph, a Levite from Cyprus?

500
What nickname did Jesus give to the disciple brothers James and John?

AKA ANSWERS

100
Paul (Acts 13:9)

200
Peter (John 1:42)

300
Daniel (Daniel 1:7)

400
Barnabas (Acts 4:36)

500
Boanerges, or Sons of Thunder (Mark 3:17)

Your Score for This Quiz:
_____Points

Cumulative Score, A Quizzes:
_____Points

"A"MEN, BROTHER

When you see a letter or word in quotation marks in the title of a quiz in *Bible Quiz Show*, you know that that letter or word will appear in the answer to those quiz questions. All of the answers to these questions are men's names starting with *A*.

Answers on next page.

100
What man, brother of Moses, was priest for the nation of Israel?

200
What Caesar ordered the census that brought Mary, expecting the baby Jesus, to Bethlehem?

300
What man, with a name like a Roman god, became a powerful preacher of Christ in the early church?

400
What Old Testament prophet was a shepherd from Tekoa?

500
What cousin of King Saul served as commander of Saul's army?

"A"MEN, BROTHER ANSWERS

100
Aaron (Exodus 4:14, 28:1)

200
Augustus (Luke 2:1–5)

300
Apollos (Acts 18:24–26)

400
Amos (Amos 1:1)

500
Abner (1 Samuel 14:51, 17:55)

Your Score for This Quiz:
_____Points

Cumulative Score, Λ Quizzes:
_____Points

ARK OF THE COVENANT

No, Indiana Jones didn't actually find the ark—that's just Hollywood hype. But the real ark of the covenant was a pretty dramatic thing itself. What do you remember about it?

Answers on next page.

100
What precious metal covered the ark and its carrying poles?

200
What leader, shortly before his death, gave orders to place the Book of the Law beside the ark?

300
Which tribe of Israel had responsibility for moving the ark?

400
What enemies of Israel captured the ark in battle?

500
What river stopped flowing when priests carrying the ark reached the water's edge?

ARK OF THE COVENANT ANSWERS

100
gold (Exodus 25:10–14)

200
Moses (Deuteronomy 31:24–26)

300
Levi (Deuteronomy 10:8)

400
the Philistines (1 Samuel 4:10–11)

500
the Jordan (Joshua 3:15–16)

Your Score for This Quiz:
_____Points

Cumulative Score, A Quizzes:
_____Points

RISK IT!

Anointing

Well, you've completed all four *A* quizzes and reached the *Risk It!* portion of the game. What do you know about biblical anointing? Consider how much of your total score on the *A* quizzes you want to risk on the one question following. If you answer correctly, you add the amount you risked to your total *A* quiz score. . .if you answer incorrectly, you *subtract* the amount you risked. Have you made your decision? Mark down the amount you're willing to risk, and we'll unveil the question. . . .

Your Total Score, A Quizzes:
_____Points

Your Risk It! Amount:
_____Points

What prophet anointed the young David as Israel's king to succeed Saul?

Answers on next page.

RISK IT! ANSWER

Samuel (1 Samuel 16:12–13)

Your Total Score, A Quizzes: _____Points

+ or - Your Risk It! Amount: _____Points

Running Total: _____Points

BAAL'S FRIENDS AND FOES

Some people loved him, and some people hated him—but he wasn't even real! What do you know about the supporters and opponents of the false god Baal?

Answers on next page.

100
What "fleecy" judge was nicknamed "Jerub-Baal" for tearing down Baal's altar?

200
What prophet of God challenged 450 prophets of Baal to see whose god would answer by fire?

300
What leader's death preceded the Israelites' descent into Baal worship?

400
What evil woman led Israel's King Ahab, her husband, into Baal worship?

500
What king of Israel claimed to worship Baal, only to destroy the priests of Baal?

BAAL'S FRIENDS AND FOES ANSWERS

100
Gideon (Judges 6:32)

200
Elijah (1 Kings 18:22–24)

300
Joshua (Judges 2:8–11)

400
Jezebel (1 Kings 16:29–31)

500
Jehu (2 Kings 10:18–19)

Your Score for This Quiz:
_____Points

BIRTHS FORETOLD

Sure, your mom knew you were coming
months before you were born. . .but
what about those Bible babies predicted
long before they were even *conceived*?
Tell us what you remember about
these special births.

Answers on next page.

100
What strongman's birth was foretold to his
father, Manoah?

200
What angel announced the birth of Jesus to His
mother, Mary?

300
What son's birth was foretold to his ninety-nine-
year-old father, Abraham?

400
What "wild donkey of a man's" birth was foretold
to his mother, Hagar?

500
What boy, destined to become king at age eight,
had his birth foretold by a man of God to the
wicked King Jeroboam?

BIRTHS FORETOLD ANSWERS

100
Samson (Judges 13:2–3, 24)

200
Gabriel (Luke 1:26–31)

300
Isaac (Genesis 18:10–11, 21:1–5)

400
Ishmael (Genesis 16:7–12)

500
Josiah (1 Kings 13:1–2)

Your Score for This Quiz:
_____Points

Cumulative Score, B Quizzes:
_____Points

BREAD

"It's the best thing since sliced bread,"
they say. Well, here's the best thing *before*
sliced bread—unsliced bread! What do
you know about bread in the Bible?

Answers on next page.

100
What two words follow Jesus' statement, "I am
the bread. . ."?

200
How many loaves of bread, along with two fish,
did Jesus turn into a meal for five thousand men?

300
What kind of bread were the Israelites to eat in
their Passover celebration?

400
What prophet requested bread from a destitute
widow—who then received a miraculous supply
of flour and oil?

500
Besides the breaking of bread, what is one of
three other things the early church devoted
itself to?

BREAD ANSWERS

100
"of life" (John 6:35)

200
five (Matthew 14:17–21)

300
unleavened (Numbers 9:10–11)

400
Elijah (1 Kings 17:9–16)

500
the apostles' teaching, fellowship, or prayer
(Acts 2:42)

Your Score for This Quiz:
_____Points

Cumulative Score, B Quizzes:
_____Points

"B"-WARE!

Those quotation marks tell you that all of the answers to these questions will start with the letter *B*. Are you ready? "B" alert now....

Answers on next page.

100
Where did God confuse the language of prideful people trying to build a tower to heaven?

200
What product were the Israelites, as slaves of Egypt, forced to make?

300
What greedy prophet was saved from death by a talking donkey?

400
What physical condition of Elisha was once mocked by young people—leading to their mauling by bears?

500
What powerful creature, described in the book of Job, has a tail that "sways like a cedar"?

"B"-WARE! ANSWERS

100
Babel (Genesis 11:1–9)

200
bricks (Exodus 5:4–8)

300
Balaam (Numbers 22:21–33)

400
baldness (2 Kings 2:23–24)

500
behemoth (Job 40:15–24)

Your Score for This Quiz:
_____Points

Cumulative Score, B Quizzes:
_____Points

RISK IT!

Barnabas

All right. . .you've navigated the *B* quizzes and it's time for another *Risk It!* question. How much do you know about Barnabas? Consider how much of your total score on the *B* quizzes you want to risk on the one question following. If you answer correctly, you add the amount you risked to your total *B* quiz score. . .if you answer incorrectly, you *subtract* the amount you risked. Ready to decide? Jot down the amount you're willing to risk, and we'll unveil the question. . . .

Your Total Score, B Quizzes:
_____Points

Your Risk It! Amount:
_____Points

What cousin of Barnabas, who temporarily deserted the ministry, caused a falling out between Barnabas and the apostle Paul?

Answer on next page.

RISK IT! ANSWER

⸻

John Mark (Acts 15:37–40)

Your Total Score, B Quizzes: _____Points

+ or - Your Risk It! Amount: _____Points

Running Total (A through B Quizzes):
_____Points

CANAAN LAND

Ah, the "promised land"—sounds peaceful and serene, doesn't it? Well, not exactly . . .Canaan Land brought its own set of challenges to the Israelites. How much do you remember from your Bible?

Answers on next page.

100
What patriarch was promised the land of Canaan by God?

200
What two foods were said to flow in the land of Canaan?

300
What leader only saw Canaan from a distance, after leading the Israelites on a forty-year journey there?

400
What disaster caused Jacob to send his sons from Canaan to Egypt?

500
What did the fearful Israelite spies who explored Canaan say they looked like compared to the giants they saw there?

CANAAN LAND ANSWERS

100
Abraham (Genesis 17:3–8)

200
milk and honey (Numbers 13:27)

300
Moses (Deuteronomy 32:48–52)

400
famine (Genesis 42:1–5)

500
grasshoppers (Numbers 13:33)

Your Score for This Quiz:
_____Points

CORINTH

Talk about staying power. . .you'll still find the city of Corinth on the map of modern Greece, two thousand years after the apostle Paul wrote letters to a church there! What do you know about their correspondence?

Answers on next page.

100
Which of these three—faith, hope, or love—did Paul say was greatest in a letter to Christians at Corinth?

200
What "prickly" physical ailment did Paul write about to the church at Corinth?

300
What man, along with his wife Priscilla, moved to Corinth from Italy when all Jews were ordered to leave Rome?

400
Who, besides Jews, did Paul preach to every Sabbath day in the Corinth synagogue?

500
What man, for whom a New Testament book is named, traveled to Corinth to help pick up an offering for needy saints?

CORINTH ANSWERS

100
love, or charity (1 Corinthians 13:13)

200
a thorn in the flesh (2 Corinthians 12:7)

300
Aquila (Acts 18:1–2)

400
Greeks (Acts 18:4)

500
Titus (2 Corinthians 8:16–19)

Your Score for This Quiz:
_____Points

Cumulative Score, C Quizzes:
_____Points

CREATIVE ANSWERS

Okay, "creative answers" is a nice way of saying "lies." There were some real whoppers told in the Bible! Show us what you know about them.

Answers on next page.

100
What disciple, watching Jesus' arrest and trial, claimed three times that he didn't know the Lord?

200
What relationship did Abram claim to his wife, Sarai, to try to gain favor with the Egyptians?

300
What did the murderous King Herod tell the wise men he wanted to do to the young boy Jesus?

400
What husband and wife died after lying about the amount of money they gave as an offering?

500
What explanation did Jewish priests and Roman soldiers give for the disappearance of Jesus' body after the Resurrection?

CREATIVE ANSWERS ANSWERS

100
Peter (Matthew 26:69–75)

200
brother to sister (Genesis 12:10–20)

300
worship Him (Matthew 2:7–8)

400
Ananias and Sapphira (Acts 5:1–11)

500
that it was stolen by the disciples (Matthew 28:11–15)

Your Score for This Quiz:
_____Points

Cumulative Score, C Quizzes:
_____Points

"C" YA

The C in this quiz title is in quotation marks—
and that's your hint that all of the answers
begin with the third letter of the alphabet.
Let's "c" how you do with these questions!

Answers on next page.

100
What did Jesus say was more likely to go through
the eye of a needle than for a rich man to enter
heaven?

200
What occupation did Joseph, Jesus' earthly
father, practice?

300
What moldable material, according to Jeremiah,
represented Israel in the hands of God?

400
What color did Isaiah use to describe sin?

500
What vegetable did the complaining Israelites
recall longingly from their years of slavery in
Egypt?

"C" YA ANSWERS

100
camel (Matthew 19:24)

200
carpentry (Matthew 13:53–55)

300
clay (Jeremiah 18:1–6)

400
crimson (Isaiah 1:18)

500
cucumbers (Numbers 11:4–5)

Your Score for This Quiz:
_____Points

Cumulative Score, C Quizzes:
_____Points

RISK IT!

Commandments

Congratulations—you've reached the *Risk It!* section for the C quizzes. Feel confident on the Ten Commandments? Decide how much of your total score on the C quizzes you want to risk on the one question following. If you answer correctly, you add the amount you risked to your total C quiz score. . .if you answer incorrectly, you *subtract* the amount you risked. Made your decision? Write down the amount you're willing to risk, and we'll unveil the question. . . .

Your Total Score, C Quizzes:
_____Points

Your Risk It! Amount:
_____Points

What issue does the last of the Ten Commandments address?

Answer on next page.

RISK IT! ANSWER

coveting (Exodus 20:17)

Your Total Score, C Quizzes:
_____ Points

+ or – Your Risk It! Amount:
_____Points

Running Total (A through C Quizzes):
_____Points

DANIEL'S STORY

Any kid in Sunday school can give
you the highlights of Daniel's story.
What do *you* know about him?

Answers on next page.

100
What illegal activity resulted in Daniel being
thrown into the lions' den?

200
What are the better-known names of Daniel's
friends Hananiah, Mishael, and Azariah?

300
What miraculous sign, interpreted by Daniel,
foretold the doom of King Belshazzar?

400
What was the composition of the feet of an
enormous statue in King Nebuchadnezzar's
dream—explained by Daniel?

500
What angel appears twice in the story of Daniel
to explain the prophet's visions?

DANIEL'S STORY ANSWERS

100
praying to God (Daniel 6:6–14)

200
Shadrach, Meshach, and Abednego (Daniel 1:7)

300
the handwriting on the wall (Daniel 5:1–31)

400
iron and clay (Daniel 2:32–33)

500
Gabriel (Daniel 8:15–16, 9:21)

Your Score for This Quiz:
_____Points

DEMONS, BEGONE

They call it an "exorcism"—making a demon (or demons) leave a possessed person. Kind of creepy, huh? It happened a lot in Bible times—how many do you recall?

Answers on next page.

100
What kind of animals rushed into a lake and drowned after receiving demons cast from humans?

200
What name did a wild man, possessed by many demons, give in answer to Jesus' question?

300
How many demons were cast out of Mary Magdalene?

400
What "skill" did a young slave girl lose when Paul cast a demon from her?

500
What specific activity did Jesus sometimes forbid to newly cast-out demons?

DEMONS, BEGONE ANSWERS

100
pigs (Matthew 8:28–32)

200
Legion (Mark 5:6–9)

300
seven (Luke 8:2)

400
fortune-telling (Acts 16:16–19)

500
speaking (Mark 1:34, Luke 4:40–41)

Your Score for This Quiz:
_____Points

Cumulative Score, D Quizzes:
_____Points

DISASTERS

Long before the *Titanic* tragedy or the San Francisco earthquake, there were major disasters in the Bible. Tell us what you know about these five.

Answers on next page.

100
What widespread lack of food forced the patriarch Isaac to leave his home and move to another country?

200
What swarming insects stripped Egypt of every green plant in the eighth plague called down by Moses?

300
What transportation disaster befell the apostle Paul as he was traveling to Rome to stand trial before Caesar?

400
What fraction of Earth's population is killed by the horses and riders of Revelation's sixth trumpet judgment?

500
What collapsed and killed eighteen people in a "news event" that Jesus used to encourage repentance?

DISASTERS ANSWERS

100
famine (Genesis 26:1)

200
locusts (Exodus 10:13–15)

300
shipwreck (Acts 27:21–44)

400
one-third (Revelation 9:13–19)

500
a tower (Luke 13:2–5)

Your Score for This Quiz:
_____Points

Cumulative Score, D Quizzes:
_____Points

"D"-TAILS

There's a set of quotation marks around that *D*, so you already have a clue as to how the answers to these five questions begin.

Answers on next page.

100
What kind of bird, released from the ark, brought an olive leaf back to Noah?

200
What substance did God use to form the first man?

300
What prophetess, the wife of Lappidoth, was a judge of Israel?

400
What did scoffers accuse the disciples of when they spoke in tongues at Pentecost?

500
What Philistine idol fell over and broke in pieces when the ark of the covenant was placed nearby?

"D"-TAILS ANSWERS

100
dove (Genesis 8:11)

200
dust (Genesis 2:7)

300
Deborah (Judges 4:4)

400
drunkenness (Acts 2:1–15)

500
Dagon (1 Samuel 5:1–5)

Your Score for This Quiz:
_____Points

Cumulative Score, D Quizzes:
_____Points

RISK IT!

Donkeys

The *D* questions are history. . . . Now it's time to *Risk It!* What do you remember about donkeys of the Bible? Choose how much of your total score on the *D* quizzes you want to risk on the one question following. If you answer correctly, you add the amount you risked to your total *D* quiz score. . .if you answer incorrectly, you *subtract* the amount you risked. Made up your mind yet? Note the amount you're willing to risk, and we'll unveil the question. . . .

Your Total Score, D Quizzes:
_____Points

Your Risk It! Amount:
_____Points

What part of a dead donkey did Samson use to kill one thousand enemy Philistines?

Answer on next page.

RISK IT! ANSWER

a jawbone (Judges 15:14–16)

Your Total Score, D Quizzes:
_____Points

+ or – Your Risk It! Amount:
_____Points

Running Total (A through D Quizzes):
_____Points

EARTHQUAKE!

Talk about shaking things up. . .
earthquakes are a relatively common
occurrence in the pages of the Bible.
How's your seismological knowledge?

Answers on next page.

100
What kind of creature started an earthquake by
rolling back the stone that sealed Jesus' tomb?

200
What mountain, where Moses received the Ten
Commandments, shook as the Lord came down
on it?

300
What missionary companion of Paul experienced
an earthquake in a Philippian jail?

400
What prophet went through an earthquake only
to learn that God spoke in a gentle whisper?

500
What is one of three miracles accompanying
the earthquake that occurred at the moment of
Jesus' death?

EARTHQUAKE! ANSWERS

100
an angel (Matthew 28:1–4)

200
Mount Sinai (Exodus 19:18–19)

300
Silas (Acts 16:25–28)

400
Elijah (1 Kings 19:11–13)

500
temple curtain torn from top to bottom; tombs broke open; bodies of dead saints raised to life (Matthew 27:50–53)

Your Score for This Quiz:
_____Points

ENGAGING STORIES

Yes, this quiz title has a double meaning—
the stories are "engaging" in that they
catch your interest. . .but they're also all
about people getting married. What do
you know about these Bible couples?

Answers on next page.

100
What man was planning to wed Mary when she
was found to be pregnant through the Holy
Spirit?

200
What woman lay at the feet of Boaz in a
threshing floor—initiating a relationship that
culminated in marriage?

300
What woman was Jacob tricked into marrying by
his devious uncle Laban?

400
What nationality of woman did Samson, to his
parents' disgust, seek out for a wife?

500
What daughter did Reuel, a priest of Midian, give
to Moses as his wife?

ENGAGING STORIES ANSWERS

100
Joseph (Matthew 1:18)

200
Ruth (Ruth 3:7–8, 4:13)

300
Leah (Genesis 29:21–23)

400
Philistine (Judges 14:1–3)

500
Zipporah (Exodus 2:16–21)

Your Score for This Quiz:
_____Points

Cumulative Score, E Quizzes:
_____Points

"E"-VENTS

And now the quotation marks surround the fifth letter of the alphabet—with every answer in this quiz starting with E. Excellent!

Answers on next page.

100
Where did God plant a garden and place the man, Adam, He had created?

200
What nationality was the man a young Moses killed and hid in the sand?

300
What kind of man did the apostle Philip find in a chariot, reading from the book of Isaiah?

400
What kind of lamb did the prophet Nathan mention in a story that exposed sin in King David's life?

500
What priestly garment did David use to ask God whether he should pursue the Amalekites, who had kidnapped two of his wives?

"E"-VENTS ANSWERS

100
Eden (Genesis 2:8)

200
Egyptian (Exodus 2:11–12)

300
Ethiopian eunuch (either answer acceptable; Acts 8:26–35)

400
ewe (2 Samuel 12:1–6)

500
ephod (1 Samuel 30:1–8)

Your Score for This Quiz:

_____Points

Cumulative Score, E Quizzes:

_____Points

EZEKIEL'S VISIONS

If you eat pizza right before bedtime, you might have some strange dreams. . .but probably nothing like the visions the prophet Ezekiel had! What do you recall of them?

Answers on next page.

100
What round objects did Ezekiel see accompanying four unusual "living creatures"?

200
What gruesome things did Ezekiel see filling a valley?

300
What heavenly body did Ezekiel see some two dozen men bowing to at the entrance to God's temple?

400
What unusual "meal" did Ezekiel eat in the vision that brought him God's calling?

500
What kind of tool did Ezekiel see a bronzed man using on a new temple on a high mountain?

EZEKIEL'S VISIONS ANSWERS

100
wheels (Ezekiel 1:15–21)

200
dry bones (Ezekiel 37:1–14)

300
the sun (Ezekiel 8:16)

400
a scroll, or the "roll of a book" (Ezekiel 2:9–3:2)

500
a measuring rod, or reed (Ezekiel 40:1–3)

Your Score for This Quiz:
_____Points

Cumulative Score, E Quizzes:
_____Points

RISK IT!

Extra-Long Words

And now you can *Risk It!* for the four
E quizzes as we test your knowledge of
extra-long words. Consider how much of
your total score on the *E* quizzes you want
to risk on the one question to follow. If you
answer correctly, you add the amount you
risked to your total *E* quiz score. . .if you
answer incorrectly, you *subtract* the amount
you risked. Settled on a number? Write
down the amount you're willing to risk,
and we'll unveil the question. . . .

Your Total Score, E Quizzes:
_____Points

Your Risk It! Amount:
_____ Points

What fourteen-letter word defined the ministry
that Paul told the Corinthians God has given
those who are in Christ?

Answer on next page.

RISK IT! ANSWER

reconciliation (2 Corinthians 5:18)

Your Total Score, E Quizzes:
_____Points

+ or – Your Risk It! Amount:
_____Points

Running Total (A through E Quizzes):
_____Points

FATHERS

They say George Washington was the "father of his country"—but who was the father of George? Here are some questions about *biblical* fathers—we'll name the kids, you name the dad.

Answers on next page.

100
Who was the father of Solomon?

200
Who was the father of Benjamin?

300
Who was the father of James and John?

400
Who was the father of Joshua?

500
Who was the father of Gershom?

FATHERS ANSWERS

100
David (2 Samuel 12:24)

200
Jacob, or Israel (Genesis 46:19)

300
Zebedee (Mark 1:19–20)

400
Nun (Numbers 11:28)

500
Moses (Exodus 2:21–22)

Your Score for This Quiz:
_____Points

FILTHY ANIMALS

"Filthy animal" isn't just an insult—it was a reality for the biblical Israelites. God called many animals "unclean," and they were not to be touched or eaten. Tell us what you know about them.

Answers on next page.

100
What kind of animal was the "prodigal son" feeding when he realized he should return home to his father?

200
What color-changing lizard was not permitted on Israelite menus?

300
What soaring bird, mentioned in Isaiah 40, led Moses' list of flying creatures that could not be eaten?

400
What bird, which brought food to Elijah, was deemed unclean in the laws of God?

500
What desert beast of burden was forbidden as food to the Israelites?

FILTHY ANIMALS ANSWERS

100
pigs (Luke 15:11–20)

200
chameleon (Leviticus 11:29–30)

300
eagle (Leviticus 11:13–19)

400
raven (1 Kings 17:1–4, Deuteronomy 14:11–14)

500
camel (Leviticus 11:4)

Your Score for This Quiz:
_____Points

Cumulative Score, F Quizzes:
_____Points

FOOD

They didn't have McDonald's back then,
but the people of the Bible loved to eat
just like we do. What do you know
about biblical foods?

Answers on next page.

100
What did Samson eat from the carcass of a lion
he had killed?

200
What insect made a large part of the diet of
John the Baptist?

300
What did Jesus eat in the presence of His
disciples shortly after His resurrection?

400
What is one of the two kinds of cakes Abigail
brought to King David to apologize for her
husband's rude behavior?

500
What kind of plants and trees did God tell Adam
and Eve they could use for food?

FOOD ANSWERS

100
honey (Judges 14:5–9)

200
locusts (Matthew 3:4)

300
broiled fish (Luke 24:36–43)

400
raisin or fig (1 Samuel 25:18–25)

500
seed bearing (Genesis 1:27–29)

Your Score for This Quiz:
_____Points

Cumulative Score, F Quizzes:
_____Points

FUTURE THINGS

You can't say what's going to happen to you tomorrow. . .but God knows the future as if it's the present. Show us your knowledge of the future things found in the Bible.

Answers on next page.

100

What did Jesus say He would arrive in when He returns to earth "with power and great glory"?

200

What special headwear will be the heavenly reward for faithful service on earth?

300

What two animals represent the saved and lost people of earth, whom Jesus will separate at the final judgment?

400

What "lake" is the final, eternal home for those people whose names are not found in the book of life?

500

How many years, according to John's Revelation, will Jesus reign on earth before Satan's final judgment?

FUTURE THINGS ANSWERS

100
a cloud (Luke 21:27)

200
a crown (2 Timothy 4:8, James 1:12)

300
sheep and goats (Matthew 25:31–33)

400
the lake of fire (Revelation 20:15)

500
one thousand (Revelation 20:6–10)

Your Score for This Quiz:
_____Points

Cumulative Score, F Quizzes:
_____Points

RISK IT!

Famous Fruit

Well, you've gotten through all four *F* quizzes and reached the *Risk It!* portion of the game. Let's test your knowledge of the "famous fruit" of the Bible. Think over how much of your total score on the *F* quizzes you want to risk on the one question following. If you answer correctly, you add the amount you risked to your total *F* quiz score. . .if you answer incorrectly, you *subtract* the amount you risked. Have you decided? Mark down the amount you're willing to risk, and we'll unveil the question. . . .

Your Total Score, F Quizzes:
_____Points

Your Risk It! Amount:
_____ Points

What is the last of the nine-fold "fruit of the spirit" mentioned in Galatians 5?

Answer on next page.

RISK IT! ANSWER

self-control, or temperance (Galatians 5:22–23)

Your Total Score, F Quizzes:
_____Points

+ or – Your Risk It! Amount:
_____Points

Running Total (A through F Quizzes):
_____Points

GOLGOTHA

You may already know that Golgotha is the place where Jesus was crucified. But what else do you know about this somber locale?

Answers on next page.

100
How many criminals were crucified with Jesus at Golgotha?

200
What part of the body completes the meaning of the name Golgotha: "The place of the. . ."?

300
How did the soldiers at Golgotha decide who should receive Jesus' clothing?

400
What did mocking soldiers offer Jesus to drink while He hung on the cross at Golgotha?

500
How many languages appeared on the sign—reading "The King of the Jews"—that hung on Jesus' cross?

GOLGOTHA ANSWERS

100
two (Mark 15:27)

200
skull (John 19:17)

300
by casting lots (John 19:23–24)

400
vinegar, or wine mixed with myrrh (Luke 23:36, Mark 15:23)

500
three (John 19:19–20)

Your Score for This Quiz:
_____Points

GOOD FOR EVIL

It's a common theme in the Bible—
paying back good for evil done. Here
are five examples. . .what do you
remember about them?

Answers on next page.

100

What did Jesus command His followers to show
to their enemies?

200

What Israelite, as a powerful official in Egypt,
forgave his brothers who years before had sold
him into slavery?

300

What did Jesus tell His disciples to do to the
people who cursed them?

400

Who did Moses ask God to heal—after God
struck her with leprosy for murmuring against
Moses' foreign wife?

500

What servant of the high priest had his ear sliced
off by Peter's sword—then restored by Jesus—
during Jesus' arrest?

GOOD FOR EVIL ANSWERS

100
love (Luke 6:35)

200
Joseph (Genesis 50:15–21)

300
bless them (Luke 6:28)

400
Miriam (Numbers 12:1–13)

500
Malchus (Luke 22:50–51, John 18:10)

Your Score for This Quiz:
_____Points

Cumulative Score, G Quizzes:
_____Points

"G" O TO

You guessed it—all of the answers in this quiz
are places that start with G. Go for it!

Answers on next page.

100
What wicked city did Jesus pair with Sodom?

200
What sea was the location of Jesus' calling of
Peter and Andrew?

300
Where did Jesus pray—and His disciples sleep—
the night He was betrayed and arrested?

400
What mount saw the deaths of King Saul and his
sons in battle?

500
What city's name appears in the name of its
"biggest" resident—Goliath?

"G"O TO ANSWERS

100
Gomorrah (Matthew 10:15)

200
Galilee (Matthew 4:18–19)

300
Gethsemane (Matthew 26:36–46)

400
Gilboa (1 Samuel 31:8)

500
Gath (1 Samuel 17:4)

Your Score for This Quiz:
_____Points

Cumulative Score, G Quizzes:
_____Points

GUILTY!

At fault, caught, busted. . .any way you look
at it, *guilty*. What do you know about these
five "cases" from the Bible?

Answers on next page.

100
Who did Adam blame when God confronted him
about eating the forbidden fruit?

200
What sin was a woman caught in by scribes and
Pharisees, who then tried to trick Jesus into
approving her death by stoning?

300
What sin against the Holy Spirit, according to
Jesus, would result in eternal guilt?

400
Who was stoned to death after admitting he had
stolen clothing, silver, and gold from the ruins of
Jericho?

500
What priests, the two sons of Eli, were judged
for treating the Lord's offerings with contempt?

GUILTY! ANSWERS

100
the woman, Eve (Genesis 3:11–12)

200
adultery (John 8:1–11)

300
blasphemy (Mark 3:28–29)

400
Achan (Joshua 7:19–25)

500
Hophni and Phinehas (1 Samuel 1:3, 2:12–17)

Your Score for This Quiz:
_____Points

Cumulative Score, G Quizzes:
_____Points

RISK IT!

Gideon

It's time to *Risk It!* for the *G* quizzes.
What do you know about Gideon?
Think about how much of your total score
on the G quizzes you want to risk on the
one question following. If you answer
correctly, you add the amount you risked
to your total G quiz score. . .if you answer
incorrectly, you *subtract* the amount you
risked. Got your number? Mark down
the amount you're willing to risk, and
we'll unveil the question. . . .

Your Total Score, G Quizzes:
_____Points

Your Risk It! Amount:
_____ Points

What substance appeared on Gideon's fleece
one night—but not the next—to convince him he
was working in God's will?

Answer on next page.

RISK IT! ANSWER

dew (Judges 6:36–40)

Your Total Score, G Quizzes:
_____Points

+ or – Your Risk It! Amount:
_____Points

Running Total (A through G Quizzes):
_____Points

HAIRY PEOPLE

There are plenty of things a person
can be known for. Here are five
Bible passages about hair. Are you
"brushed up" on this category?

Answers on next page.

100
What Bible strongman lost his power when his
long hair was cut off?

200
What twin brother of Jacob was born hairy?

300
What son of David cut his long hair whenever it
became too heavy for him?

400
What did the apostle Paul say that long hair is to
a woman?

500
What does the "lover" in the Song of Songs
twice compare his "beloved's" hair to?

HAIRY PEOPLE ANSWERS

100
Samson (Judges 16:15–20)

200
Esau (Genesis 25:25–26)

300
Absalom (2 Samuel 14:25–26)

400
glory (1 Corinthians 11:15)

500
a flock of goats (Song of Songs 4:1, 6:5)

Your Score for This Quiz:
_____Points

HEAVENLY SOUNDS

Now hear this. . . . The Bible tells of many different sounds from heaven. What do you know about the five following?

Answers on next page.

100
What event in Jesus' life featured a voice from heaven saying, "This is my Son, whom I love"?

200
What sound from heaven accompanied God's work at Pentecost?

300
What musical instrument accompanies the song of victorious saints in heaven, according to John's Revelation?

400
What sound, according to the apostle Paul, causes every knee in heaven to bow?

500
What does the voice of the "living creature" resemble when the Lamb breaks the first seal on the seven-sealed book of Revelation?

HEAVENLY SOUNDS ANSWERS

100
His baptism (Matthew 3:16–17)

200
a violent, or mighty, wind (Acts 2:1–4)

300
harps (Revelation 15:1–4)

400
the name of Jesus (Philippians 2:10)

500
thunder (Revelation 5:1, 6:1)

Your Score for This Quiz:
_____Points

Cumulative Score, H Quizzes:
_____Points

"H"ELLO THERE

The *H* in quotation marks means every answer will start with that letter. And here's another hint: Each answer is a person's name. . . .

Answers on next page.

100
What woman, the wife of Elkanah, was mother of the prophet Samuel?

200
What Old Testament prophet, at God's command, married an adulterous woman named Gomer?

300
What wicked New Testament king "was eaten by worms and died" for allowing people to call him a god?

400
What king of Tyre supplied cedar logs to Solomon for building the Lord's temple?

500
What prophetess told the faithful King Josiah he would not see the disaster God was bringing on his unfaithful nation?

"H"ELLO THERE ANSWERS

100
Hannah (1 Samuel 1:19–20)

200
Hosea (Hosea 1:2–3)

300
Herod (Acts 12:21–23)

400
Hiram (1 Kings 5:1–12)

500
Huldah (2 Kings 22:14–20)

Your Score for This Quiz:
_____Points

Cumulative Score, H Quizzes:
_____Points

"HOLY," HOLY, HOLY

You'll note that the word *holy* is in
quotation marks—so every answer
will be a phrase featuring that word.

Answers on next page.

100
What did Jesus promise that God the Father
would give to anyone who asked?

200
What did God tell Moses he was standing on
when he approached the burning bush?

300
What did John call the new Jerusalem he saw in
a vision, coming down out of heaven?

400
What did Paul tell Timothy that Christians should
lift up in prayer?

500
What four-word phrase is used often in the book
of Isaiah to describe the Lord?

"HOLY," HOLY, HOLY ANSWERS

100
the Holy Spirit (Luke 11:11–13)

200
holy ground (Exodus 3:3–5)

300
the Holy City (Revelation 21:1–2)

400
holy hands (1 Timothy 2:8)

500
"Holy One of Israel" (see, for example, Isaiah 49:7)

Your Score for This Quiz:
_____Points

Cumulative Score, H Quizzes:
_____Points

RISK IT!

Hard Labor

All right. . .you've completed the *H* quizzes, and it's time to *Risk It!* How confident are you on the category "Hard Labor"? Consider how much of your total score on the *H* quizzes you want to risk on the one question following. If you answer correctly, you add the amount you risked to your total *H* quiz score. . .if you answer incorrectly, you *subtract* the amount you risked. Are you ready? Write down the amount you're willing to risk, and we'll unveil the question. . . .

Your Total Score, H Quizzes:
_____Points

Your Risk It! Amount:
_____ Points

What body fluid was part of the curse that came by Adam and Eve's sin?

Answer on next page.

RISK IT! ANSWER

sweat (Genesis 3:19)

Your Total Score, H Quizzes:
_____Points

+ or – Your Risk It! Amount:
_____Points

Running Total (A through H Quizzes):
_____Points

"I" KNOW

We certainly hope you know these answers,
which all begin with the letter *I*. Go ahead—
impress us with your intellect!

Answers on next page.

100
What lodging place in Bethlehem turned away
Joseph and his very expectant wife, Mary?

200
What metal, used to sharpen other like metal,
does Proverbs compare to friends?

300
What kind of place was Patmos, where John
received his Revelation of Jesus Christ?

400
What major prophet had a son named Shear-
Jashub?

500
What does the apostle Paul urge Christians to be
". . .of God"?

"I" KNOW ANSWERS

100
inn (Luke 2:4–7 KJV)

200
iron (Proverbs 27:17)

300
Island, or isle (Revelation 1:9)

400
Isaiah (Isaiah 7:3)

500
imitators (Ephesians 5:1 KJV)

Your Score for This Quiz:
_____Points

IMPRISONED

Long before Monopoly popularized the "Get Out of Jail Free" card, these Bible characters found themselves stuck in a jail cell without one! What do you know about their stories?

Answers on next page.

100
What handsome son of Jacob was imprisoned after a false report from Potiphar's wife?

200
What wandering preacher was imprisoned for challenging the adulterous marriage of King Herod?

300
What notorious prisoner gained his freedom from Pontius Pilate as Jesus was sentenced to crucifixion?

400
What "weeping prophet" was imprisoned in a dungeon on false charges of deserting to the enemy?

500
What two things were Paul and Silas doing at midnight while imprisoned in a Philippian jail?

IMPRISONED ANSWERS

100
Joseph (Genesis 39:2–20)

200
John the Baptist (Mark 6:14–18)

300
Barabbas (Matthew 27:16–26)

400
Jeremiah (Jeremiah 37:12–16)

500
praying and singing to God (Acts 16:22–25)

Your Score for This Quiz:
_____Points

Cumulative Score, I Quizzes:
_____Points

INSECTS

Don't let this category bug you. . . .
All you need to do is answer five questions
involving insects in the Bible.

Answers on next page.

100
What hardworking insect does the book of
Proverbs tell lazy people to learn from?

200
What insects are mentioned by the writer of the
book of James as destroyers of clothing?

300
What insect swarmed Egypt in the fourth plague
on Pharaoh—but stayed out of the land of
Goshen where God's people lived?

400
What tiny insect did Jesus say the hypocritical
Pharisees strained out of their food, only to
"swallow a camel"?

500
What stinging insect did God use to drive enemy
peoples out of the Promised Land?

INSECTS ANSWERS

100
ants (Proverbs 6:6–8)

200
moths (James 5:2)

300
flies (Exodus 8:20–24)

400
gnat (Matthew 23:23–24)

500
hornet (Joshua 24:11–12)

Your Score for This Quiz:
_____Points

Cumulative Score, I Quizzes:
_____Points

ISAAC

We're not talking about the hymn writer,
Watts; the scientist, Newton; or the
science-fiction wiz, Asimov. . . . The Isaac
in this category is a biblical patriarch.
How well do you know his story?

Answers on next page.

100
What "father of many nations" was first of all
father to Isaac?

200
What did Isaac's elderly mother, Sarah, do when
she was told she would give birth to Isaac?

300
What was the name of Isaac's older half-brother?

400
Where did God tell Isaac's father to sacrifice the
young man as a burnt offering?

500
What did the Philistines, envious of Isaac's
wealth in flocks and herds, try to destroy?

ISAAC ANSWERS

100
Abraham (Genesis 17:5, 21:3)

200
laugh (Genesis 18:10–12)

300
Ishmael (Genesis 25:12)

400
Moriah (Genesis 22:1–2)

500
wells (Genesis 26:12–15)

Your Score for This Quiz:
_____Points

Cumulative Score, I Quizzes:
_____Points

RISK IT!

Initials

Here we are at the *Risk It!* category for the four *I* quizzes. Let's test your knowledge of initials of the Bible. Decide how much of your total score on the *I* quizzes you want to risk on the one question following. If you answer correctly, you add the amount you risked to your total *I* quiz score. . .if you answer incorrectly, you *subtract* the amount you risked. Have a figure in mind? Mark down the amount you're willing to risk, and we'll unveil the question. . . .

Your Total Score, I Quizzes:
_____Points

Your Risk It! Amount:
_____ Points

Who is J. of A.—a secret disciple who cared for Jesus' body after the crucifixion?

Answer on next page.

RISK IT! ANSWER

//

Joseph of Arimathea (John 19:38–42)

Your Total Score, I Quizzes:
_____Points

+ or – Your Risk It! Amount:
_____Points

Running Total (A through I Quizzes):
_____Points

JESSE'S BOYS

Way back in Bible times, a man named
Jesse had several sons. Tell us what
you know about Jesse's boys.

Answers on next page.

100
What youngest boy of Jesse was anointed by the
prophet Samuel to be king?

200
What town, where years later Jesus would be
born, was home to Jesse's boys?

300
What enemies were Jesse's oldest boys, as
members of the Israelite army, opposing in the
Valley of Elah?

400
How many boys in all did Jesse have?

500
Who was Jesse's firstborn boy?

JESSE'S BOYS ANSWERS

100
David (1 Samuel 16:13)

200
Bethlehem (1 Samuel 17:58)

300
Philistines (1 Samuel 17:17–19)

400
eight (1 Samuel 16:10–11)

500
Eliab (1 Samuel 17:28)

Your Score for This Quiz:
_____Points

JEWELS

They say that diamonds are a girl's best friend. . .but God must like jewels too. What do you recall of the precious stones scattered through the pages of the Bible?

Answers on next page.

100
What valuable red stones, according to Proverbs, are worth less than either wisdom or a good wife?

200
What green stone resembles the rainbow circling God's throne in heaven?

300
How many precious stones, representing the tribes of Israel, were part of the breastplate worn by Old Testament priests?

400
What jewel did Jesus warn against throwing to pigs?

500
What part of the city wall of the New Jerusalem is decorated with precious stones?

JEWELS ANSWERS

100
rubies (Proverbs 8:11, 31:10)

200
emerald (Revelation 4:1–3)

300
twelve (Exodus 28:15–21)

400
pearls (Matthew 7:6)

500
the foundations (Revelation 21:1–21)

Your Score for This Quiz:
_____Points

Cumulative Score, J Quizzes:
_____Points

JOB

You probably know something about the suffering saint named Job. . .but do you know enough to complete this quiz? Let's find out!

Answers on next page.

100
What accuser received God's permission to attack Job's possessions, family, and health?

200
What four words of (bad) advice did Job's wife have for her husband?

300
How did Job, defending God's right to give and take away, describe himself upon entering and departing this world?

400
What was the two-letter name of Job's homeland?

500
What trio of friends offered Job plenty of advice but little comfort throughout his trials?

JOB ANSWERS

100
Satan (Job 1:12, 2:6–7)

200
"Curse God and die" (Job 2:9)

300
naked (Job 1:20–22)

400
Uz (Job 1:1)

500
Eliphaz, Bildad, and Zophar (Job 2:11 and following)

Your Score for This Quiz:
_____Points

Cumulative Score, J Quizzes:
_____Points

"J"-WALKING

Okay, we're making this easy for you.
The quotation marks give you an automatic
hint to the answers to these questions:
They'll all start with the letter *J*.

Answers on next page.

100

What was the first name of the traitorous
disciple Iscariot?

200

What son of Saul loved his friend David "as
himself"?

300

What synagogue official saw his twelve-year-old
daughter raised to life by Jesus?

400

What priest of Midian was father-in-law to
Moses?

500

What woman helped Deborah earn a complete
military victory by driving a tent peg through
the head of the sleeping enemy commander,
Sisera?

"J"-WALKING ANSWERS

100
Judas (Luke 6:16)

200
Jonathan (1 Samuel 18:1)

300
Jairus (Luke 8:41–56)

400
Jethro (Exodus 3:1)

500
Jael (Judges 4:17–21)

Your Score for This Quiz:
_____Points

Cumulative Score, J Quizzes:
_____Points

RISK IT!

Judge and Jury

You've gotten through the *J* quizzes. . .
and now you'll *Risk It!* How does this
"Judge and Jury" category sound to you?
Think over how much of your total score
on the *J* quizzes you want to risk on the
one question following. If you answer
correctly, you add the amount you risked
to your total *J* quiz score. . .if you answer
incorrectly, you *subtract* the amount you
risked. Have a figure in mind? Mark down
the amount you're willing to risk, and
we'll unveil the question. . . .

Your Total Score, J Quizzes:
_____Points

Your Risk It! Amount:
_____ Points

What two words describe the throne on which
God sits while passing final judgment on those
who have died?

Answer on next page.

RISK IT! ANSWER

"great white" (Revelation 20:11)

Your Total Score, J Quizzes:
_____Points

+ or – Your Risk It! Amount:
_____Points

Running Total (A through J Quizzes):
_____Points

KINGDOM OF HEAVEN

Jesus had a lot to say about the kingdom of heaven—what it's like, where you find it, who's a part of it. How well do you remember His words?

Answers on next page.

100
What tiny seed did Jesus liken the kingdom of heaven to?

200
What door-openers to the kingdom of heaven did Jesus say He would give to Peter?

300
What group of people, whom the disciples tried to keep from Jesus, did Jesus say are true possessors of the kingdom of heaven?

400
What repetitive phrase, according to Jesus, will not guarantee entry into the kingdom of heaven?

500
What two groups, according to Jesus in the Beatitudes, would inherit the kingdom of heaven?

KINGDOM OF HEAVEN ANSWERS

100
mustard (Matthew 13:31–32)

200
keys (Matthew 16:15–19)

300
little children (Matthew 19:14)

400
"Lord, Lord" (Matthew 7:21)

500
the poor in spirit, those persecuted for righteousness (Matthew 5:3, 10)

Your Score for This Quiz:
_____Points

KINGS OF EARTH

We're not talking Burger King, here. . .we want to know what you know about the men who ruled the nations of Bible times.

Answers on next page.

100
Which apostle defended himself before a king named Agrippa—and tried to convert him in the process?

200
What king unwittingly signed a decree that caused his friend, Daniel, to be thrown into a den of lions?

300
What prophet had a dramatic vision and calling from God in the year that King Uzziah died?

400
What king of Persia permitted the Jews in his realm to return to Jerusalem to rebuild the temple?

500
What king of Gath fell for David's trick of feigning insanity—and let him go free?

KINGS OF EARTH ANSWERS

100
Paul (Acts 25:13–26:28)

200
Darius (Daniel 6:1–16)

300
Isaiah (Isaiah 6:1–8)

400
Cyrus (Ezra 1:1–4)

500
Achish (1 Samuel 21:10–15)

Your Score for This Quiz:
_____Points

Cumulative Score, K Quizzes:
_____Points

KISS ME

They weren't always romantic, but there are several stories of kisses in the Bible. What do you recall about the following?

Answers on next page.

100
What disciple betrayed Jesus with a kiss?

200
What best friend of David kissed him when David fled from King Saul?

300
What part of Jesus' body did a sinful woman anoint with perfume and kiss during a dinner at a Pharisee's house?

400
What future wife did Jacob kiss the first time he met her—as she watered a flock of sheep?

500
What kind of kiss did the apostle Paul tell the Corinthians to greet each other with?

KISS ME ANSWERS

100
Judas Iscariot (Mark 14:43–45, John 6:70–71)

200
Jonathan (1 Samuel 20:41–42)

300
His feet (Luke 7:36–38)

400
Rachel (Genesis 29:9–11)

500
holy (1 Corinthians 16:20, 2 Corinthians 13:12)

Your Score for This Quiz:
_____Points

Cumulative Score, K Quizzes:
_____Points

KNOCK, KNOCK

No, it's not the opening of a silly joke. In this category, you'll need to show your knowledge of "knocking" in the Bible.

Answers on next page.

100

What two commands on prayer, besides "knock," did Jesus give during His Sermon on the Mount?

200

What servant girl, in her excitement at learning Peter was out of prison and at the door, left him knocking while she ran to tell the other disciples?

300

What did Jesus say servants should be doing when their master, returning from a wedding banquet, knocked on the door?

400

What did Jesus tell church members in Laodicea He would do with them if they opened the door to His knocking?

500

What kind of knocking accompanied the handwriting on the wall that terrified the Babylonian king Belshazzar?

KNOCK, KNOCK ANSWERS

100
ask and seek (Matthew 7:7–8)

200
Rhoda (Acts 12:12–16)

300
watching (Luke 12:35–38)

400
eat with them (Revelation 3:20)

500
the knocking together of the king's knees
(Daniel 5:1–6)

Your Score for This Quiz:
_____Points

Cumulative Score, K Quizzes:
_____Points

RISK IT!

Kneeling

It's time again to *Risk It!*—this time, for your score on the four *K* quizzes. We're talking about kneeling in the Bible. Decide how much of your total score on the *K* quizzes you want to risk on the one question following. If you answer correctly, you add the amount you risked to your total *K* quiz score. . .if you answer incorrectly, you *subtract* the amount you risked. Are you ready? Jot down the amount you're willing to risk, and we'll unveil the question. . . .

Your Total Score, K Quizzes:
_____Points

Your Risk It! Amount:
_____ Points

What woman, also known as Tabitha, was raised from the dead after Peter knelt and prayed?

Answer on next page.

RISK IT! ANSWER

‖‖

Dorcas (Acts 9:36–41)

Your Total Score, K Quizzes:
_____Points

+ or – Your Risk It! Amount:
_____Points

Running Total (A through K Quizzes):
_____Points

LAND

Long before there were real estate agents, people were surveying, buying, and selling land. Tell us what you know about these cases.

Answers on next page.

100
Who did God say should have first inheritance rights to the property of a man who died without sons?

200
What did the law forbid Israelites to do to their neighbors' "landmarks," or boundary stones?

300
Which tribe of Israel, set apart to be priests, did not receive part of the Promised Land, since "the LORD is their inheritance"?

400
What field was purchased by the chief priests with the "blood money" they got back from a remorseful Judas Iscariot?

500
What special celebration, every fifty years, saw property that had been sold returned to its original owners?

LAND ANSWERS

100
his daughters (Numbers 27:1–8)

200
move, or remove, them (Deuteronomy 19:14)

300
the Levites (Joshua 18:3–7)

400
the potter's field (Matthew 27:3–7)

500
Jubilee (Leviticus 25:28)

Your Score for This Quiz:
_____Points

LEVITICUS

Leviticus is the Old Testament rule book. But you'll also find some stories inside, usually of people who broke those rules. How much do you know about this third book of the Bible?

Answers on next page.

100
What body fluid did God forbid the Israelites to eat because it holds the life of every creature?

200
What was the method of execution for a man who blasphemed the Lord's name with a curse?

300
What is one of the two kinds of birds a poor person could substitute for a lamb when making sacrifice for sin?

400
What term, meaning "one who bears blame," described a sacrificial goat chosen by lot to be set free in the desert?

500
What two sons of Aaron were burned to death for offering unauthorized fire to the Lord?

LEVITICUS ANSWERS

100
blood (Leviticus 17:13–14)

200
stoning (Leviticus 24:10–23)

300
dove or pigeon (Leviticus 5:6–7)

400
scapegoat (Leviticus 16:6–10)

500
Nadab and Abihu (Leviticus 10:1–2)

Your Score for This Quiz:
_____Points

Cumulative Score, L Quizzes:
_____Points

LOVELY PEOPLE

Call them the Bible's supermodels. . . .
What do you know about these lovely
ladies—and one handsome man—
from the pages of scripture?

Answers on next page.

100

What beautiful woman was the wife of Abram,
later known as Abraham?

200

What future Israelite leader, as a baby, was
described as "no ordinary child" or "exceeding
fair" (KJV)?

300

What Old Testament queen was deposed and
later replaced by Esther when she refused to
parade her beauty at a royal banquet?

400

What beautiful daughter of David was
mistreated by her stepbrother Amnon—who
paid for that sin with his life?

500

What intelligent and beautiful woman, the wife
of the surly Nabal, married King David after
Nabal died?

LOVELY PEOPLE ANSWERS

100
Sarai, later known as Sarah (Genesis 12:11, 17:15)

200
Moses (Acts 7:20)

300
Vashti (Esther 1:10–19)

400
Tamar (2 Samuel 13:1–14, 28–29)

500
Abigail (1 Samuel 25:3, 39–42)

Your Score for This Quiz:
_____Points

Cumulative Score, L Quizzes:
_____Points

LUKE

Linus quoted him at length in *The Charlie Brown Christmas Special*. . .not bad for a guy who wrote almost two thousand years ago. What else do you know about the biblical writer Luke?

Answers on next page.

100
What professional title, besides missionary, did Luke hold?

200
What group of people, according to Luke, received the angels' announcement of the birth of Jesus?

300
What young man, who fell from a window and died during a sermon by the apostle Paul, is described in Luke's book of Acts?

400
What are two of the four ways Luke says the young boy Jesus grew up?

500
To whom did Luke address the New Testament books of Luke and Acts?

LUKE ANSWERS

100
doctor (Colossians 4:14)

200
shepherds (Luke 2:8–15)

300
Eutychus (Acts 20:7–12)

400
in wisdom, stature, favor with God, and favor with men (Luke 2:52)

500
Theophilus (Luke 1:3, Acts 1:1)

Your Score for This Quiz:
_____Points

Cumulative Score, L Quizzes:
_____Points

RISK IT!

Liberty

The four *L* quizzes are now in the books. . .
and it's your opportunity to *Risk It!* How
does a category on "Liberty" sound?
Consider how much of your total score on
the *L* quizzes you want to risk on the one
question to follow. If you answer correctly,
you add the amount you risked to your total
L quiz score. . .if you answer incorrectly, you
subtract the amount you risked. Are you
ready? Mark down the amount you're willing
to risk, and we'll unveil the question. . . .

Your Total Score, L Quizzes:
_____Points

Your Risk It! Amount:
_____ Points

What, according to Jesus, would set free the
crowds who followed Him?

Answer on next page.

RISK IT! ANSWER

the truth (John 8:31–32)

Your Total Score, L Quizzes:
_____Points

+ or – Your Risk It! Amount:
_____Points

Running Total (A through L Quizzes):
_____Points

"M"ANY ARE CALLED

There they are again—the quotation marks in the quiz title. Every answer in this quiz will be a person's name starting with *M*.

Answers on next page.

100
What leader of Israel had a staff, or rod, that turned into a snake?

200
What woman complained when her sister Mary chose to spend time with the visiting Jesus rather than help with housework?

300
What man, cousin of Queen Esther, served as her advisor and saved the Jews from destruction?

400
What man was chosen by lot to be the twelfth disciple in place of the departed Judas Iscariot?

500
What firstborn son of Joseph received a lesser blessing than his younger brother Ephraim from his grandfather Jacob?

"M"ANY ARE CALLED ANSWERS

100
Moses (Exodus 4:1–4)

200
Martha (Luke 10:38–42)

300
Mordecai (Esther 2:7, 10:3)

400
Matthias (Acts 1:23–26)

500
Manasseh (Genesis 48:17–20)

Your Score for This Quiz:
_____Points

MATTHEW'S GOSPEL

Most of us already know that there are
four Gospels in the New Testament—
but what do you know about stories
that appear *only* in Matthew's Gospel?

Answers on next page.

100

What visitors, carrying gifts for the young child
Jesus, are noted only in Matthew's Gospel?

200

What gem "of great value" did Jesus mention in
a parable found only in Matthew's Gospel?

300

What form of suicide used by Judas Iscariot is
mentioned only in Matthew's Gospel?

400

What fishing tool did Jesus liken to the kingdom
of heaven in a parable found only in Matthew's
Gospel?

500

What country did Joseph, Mary, and the baby
Jesus flee to for safety from King Herod, in an
account found only in Matthew's Gospel?

MATTHEW'S GOSPEL ANSWERS

100
Magi, or wise men (Matthew 2:1–2)

200
pearl (Matthew 13:45–46)

300
hanging (Matthew 27:5)

400
a net (Matthew 13:47–50)

500
Egypt (Matthew 2:13)

Your Score for This Quiz:
_____Points

Cumulative Score, M Quizzes:
_____Points

MIRACLES

They don't call them "miracles" for nothing.
. . . Tell us what you know about these
amazing stories from the Bible.

Answers on next page.

100
What city's walls fell at the shout of Joshua's army?

200
What did Jesus, in His first recorded miracle, change into wine?

300
In what town did Elijah bring a widow's son back to life?

400
What river divided when the prophet Elisha struck it with Elijah's cloak?

500
What two cloth items, after being touched by the apostle Paul, were used to heal the sick and drive out demons?

MIRACLES ANSWERS

100
Jericho (Joshua 6:2–5, 20)

200
water (John 2:1–11)

300
Zarephath (1 Kings 17:8–22)

400
the Jordan (2 Kings 2:12–14)

500
handkerchiefs and aprons (Acts 19:11–12)

Your Score for This Quiz:
_____Points

Cumulative Score, M Quizzes:
_____Points

MOUNTS AND MOUNTAINS

Everest, McKinley, and the Matterhorn don't appear in the Bible, but several other mounts and mountains do. What do you remember about the following?

Answers on next page.

100
What mountain chain was the final stopping point for Noah's ark?

200
What mount is associated with the heavenly Jerusalem?

300
What mountain did Moses climb to see the Promised Land he would not be allowed to enter?

400
What mountain was the setting for Moses' encounter with God in a burning bush?

500
What well-known Bible character died on Mount Hor?

MOUNTS AND MOUNTAINS ANSWERS

100
Ararat (Genesis 8:1–4)

200
Zion, or Sion (Hebrews 12:22)

300
Pisgah (Deuteronomy 3:21–29)

400
Horeb (Exodus 3:1–6)

500
Aaron (Numbers 33:39)

Your Score for This Quiz:
_____Points

Cumulative Score, M Quizzes:
_____Points

RISK IT!

Magical Moments

We've now reached the *Risk It!* question for the M quizzes. . .and "Magical Moments" sounds interesting. Think about how much of your total score on the M quizzes you want to risk on the one question following. If you answer correctly, you add the amount you risked to your total M quiz score. . .if you answer incorrectly, you *subtract* the amount you risked. Have you determined your number? Write down the amount you're willing to risk, and we'll unveil the question. . . .

Your Total Score, M Quizzes:
_____Points

Your Risk It! Amount:
_____ Points

What prophet did King Saul have a medium at Endor call up from the dead?

Answer on next page.

RISK IT! ANSWER

▏▏

Samuel (1 Samuel 28:3–15)

Your Total Score, M Quizzes:
_____Points

+ or – Your Risk It! Amount:
_____Points

Running Total (A through M Quizzes):
_____Points

NIGHTTIME

Even before electric lighting, nighttime
was a busy time for people in the Bible.
What do you know about these
nighttime experiences?

Answers on next page.

100
Which day of creation included God making
night?

200
What prophet, troubled by King Saul's
waywardness, cried out all night long to God?

300
What supernatural source of nighttime light led
the Israelites on their journey out of Egypt?

400
Where was Paul, experiencing a nighttime vision
of a man, invited to spread the gospel?

500
What sin did the apostle Paul tell the
Thessalonians is likely to occur at night?

NIGHTTIME ANSWERS

100
the first (Genesis 1:5)

200
Samuel (1 Samuel 15:10–11)

300
a pillar of fire (Exodus 13:18–22)

400
Macedonia (Acts 16:9–10)

500
drunkenness (1 Thessalonians 5:7)

Your Score for This Quiz:
_____Points

NINEVEH

It may have been the New York City of its time—Nineveh was an important place in need of God. . . . Can you recall its story well enough to answer these questions?

Answers on next page.

100
What prophet tried to disobey God's call to preach to Nineveh—and was waylaid by a giant fish?

200
How many days' warning of the destruction to come did God give Nineveh?

300
What mournful clothing did the people of Nineveh wear to show their repentance before God?

400
Of 12,000, 120,000, or 1.2 million, what was the approximate population of what God called the "great city" of Nineveh?

500
What "mighty hunter" built Nineveh shortly after Noah's time?

NINEVEH ANSWERS

100
Jonah (Jonah 1:1–3, 17)

200
forty (Jonah 3:4)

300
sackcloth (Jonah 3:5)

400
120,000 (Jonah 4:11)

500
Nimrod (Genesis 10:8–11)

Your Score for This Quiz:
_____Points

Cumulative Score, N Quizzes:
_____Points

"N"-JOY

You see those quotation marks around the letter *N*. . .so you know what each answer will begin with. Now get to it!

Answers on next page.

100
Who built an ark to save his family and every type of animal from a worldwide flood?

200
Who did Jesus tell an expert in the Law he should love as himself?

300
What wall-building Jewish exile has a book of the Old Testament named for him?

400
What kind of man was Samson, who was never to cut his hair?

500
What disciple first responded to news of the Messiah by saying, "Nazareth! Can anything good come from there?"

"N"-JOY ANSWERS

100
Noah (Genesis 6)

200
(his) neighbor (Matthew 22:34–39)

300
Nehemiah (Nehemiah 1–2:8)

400
Nazirite (Judges 13)

500
Nathanael (John 1:43–51)

Your Score for This Quiz:
_____Points

Cumulative Score, N Quizzes:
_____Points

NUMBER, NUMBER

Have you been keeping count?
The Bible is full of numbers. . . .
Can you remember these?

Answers on next page.

100
How many days did God use to create the world and everything in it?

200
How many men did Moses send into Canaan to spy out the land?

300
How many days was Lazarus in the grave before being resurrected?

400
What, according to Revelation, is the "number of the beast"?

500
How many silver coins did Judas Iscariot receive for betraying Jesus?

NUMBER, NUMBER ANSWERS

100
six (Genesis 1:31–2:1)

200
twelve (Numbers 13:1–15)

300
four (John 11:17)

400
666 (Revelation 13:18)

500
thirty (Matthew 27:3–4)

Your Score for This Quiz:
_____Points

Cumulative Score, N Quizzes:
_____Points

RISK IT!

New Birth

Well, you've completed all four *N* quizzes and reached the *Risk It!* portion of the game. What do you know about the new birth? Consider how much of your total score on the *N* quizzes you want to risk on the one question following. If you answer correctly, you add the amount you risked to your total *N* quiz score. . .if you answer incorrectly, you *subtract* the amount you risked. Have you made your decision? Mark down the amount you're willing to risk, and we'll unveil the question. . . .

Your Total Score, N Quizzes:
_____Points

Your Risk It! Amount:
_____ Points

What Jewish ruler was told by Jesus, "You must be born again"?

Answer on next page.

RISK IT! ANSWER

Nicodemus (John 3:1–7)

Your Total Score, N Quizzes:
_____Points

+ or – Your Risk It! Amount:
_____Points

Running Total (A through N Quizzes):
_____Points

OCCUPATIONS

That's the big word for "jobs"—
and Bible people had them just like
we do today. Tell us what you know
about these ancient occupations.

Answers on next page.

100

What was Matthew's job before he became a disciple of Jesus?

200

What job did the youthful David have before his anointing as king?

300

Who was one of the two royal employees who shared a jail cell with the falsely accused Joseph?

400

What occupation did the apostle Paul have in addition to his missionary duties?

500

What was the occupation of the man Demetrius, a devotee of the goddess Artemis, also known as Diana?

OCCUPATIONS ANSWERS

100
tax collector (Matthew 9:9)

200
shepherd (1 Samuel 16:11–13)

300
cupbearer (or butler) and baker (Genesis 40)

400
tentmaker (Acts 18:1–3)

500
silversmith (Acts 19:24)

Your Score for This Quiz:
_____Points

OLD PEOPLE

None of us are getting any younger,
you know. What can you recall
about the elderly in the Bible?

Answers on next page.

100

What color hair, according to the Proverbs, is
the "splendor of the old"?

200

What man lived the longest life recorded in the
Bible—969 years?

300

What son of Jared lived "only" 365 years but
didn't die—because God took him away?

400

What elderly prophetess met Mary, Joseph, and
the baby Jesus at the temple and thanked God
for the redemption to come?

500

How old was Noah when God sent the flood to
destroy the earth?

OLD PEOPLE ANSWERS

100
gray (Proverbs 20:29)

200
Methuselah (Genesis 5:27)

300
Enoch (Genesis 5:18, 23–24, Hebrews 11:5)

400
Anna (Luke 2:36–38)

500
six hundred (Genesis 7:11)

Your Score for This Quiz:
_____Points

Cumulative Score, O Quizzes:
_____Points

"O" MY!

Okay, here's a category where all the answers start with the letter O. Onward!

Answers on next page.

100
What "Mount of" was frequented by Jesus?

200
What Greek letter did Jesus pair with "Alpha" to describe Himself?

300
What kind of tree caught Absalom's long hair as he rode underneath on a mule, leaving him hanging?

400
What did Samuel tell King Saul is better than sacrifice?

500
What widowed woman left her mother-in-law, Naomi, and sister-in-law, Ruth, to return to her homeland of Moab?

"O" MY! ANSWERS

100
Olives (Luke 22:39)

200
Omega (Revelation 22:12–13)

300
oak (2 Samuel 18:9–10)

400
(to) obey (1 Samuel 15:22–25)

500
Orpah (Ruth 1:3–5, 14–15)

Your Score for This Quiz:
_____Points

Cumulative Score, O Quizzes:
_____Points

ONCE UPON A RHYME

Yes, this is a silly category. . . . You'll need
to combine two rhyming words to provide
the answers to these questions.

Answers on next page.

100
What did the first woman sew together to hide
her nakedness?

200
What would you call the king of Israel who stood
head and shoulders above everyone else?

300
What would you call flowers of Sharon
belonging to the Ten Commandments man?

400
What did the apostle Paul say some Christians
might do to the detriment of less mature
believers?

500
What might you call the flames the disciple
Cephas used to warm himself the night of Jesus'
arrest?

ONCE UPON A RHYME ANSWERS

100
Eve's leaves (Genesis 3:1–20)

200
Tall Saul (1 Samuel 9:2)

300
Moses' roses (Exodus 20:1–21, Song of Songs 2:1)

400
eat meat (1 Corinthians 8:4–13)

500
Peter's heaters (John 1:42, Luke 22:54–55)

Your Score for This Quiz:
_____Points

Cumulative Score, O Quizzes:
_____Points

RISK IT!

Onesimus

All right. . .you've navigated the *O* quizzes and it's time for another *Risk It!* question. How much do you know about Onesimus? Consider how much of your total score on the *O* quizzes you want to risk on the one question following. If you answer correctly, you add the amount you risked to your total *O* quiz score. . .if you answer incorrectly, you *subtract* the amount you risked. Ready to decide? Jot down the amount you're willing to risk, and we'll unveil the question. . . .

Your Total Score, O Quizzes:
_____Points

Your Risk It! Amount:
_____ Points

What was the relationship of Onesimus to the New Testament letter recipient Philemon?

Answer on next page.

RISK IT! ANSWER

slave (Philemon 10–16)

Your Total Score, O Quizzes:
_____Points

+ or – Your Risk It! Amount:
_____Points

Running Total (A through O Quizzes):
_____Points

PASSOVER

The Jews have been commemorating
the Passover for thousands of years now.
What do you know about its origins?

Answers on next page.

100
What kind of animal did God tell the Israelites to slaughter and eat during the Passover?

200
Where were the Israelites to apply some of the blood from the Passover sacrifice?

300
Who was to die in Egyptian households on the night of Passover?

400
What baking product was banned from Israelite homes for an entire week during the Passover celebration?

500
What was the requirement for male slaves and foreigners to eat the Passover meal?

PASSOVER ANSWERS

100
a lamb (Exodus 12:3–6)

200
to their doorframes (Exodus 12:7)

300
the firstborn (Exodus 12:12–13)

400
yeast, or leaven (Exodus 12:19)

500
circumcision (Exodus 12:43–49)

Your Score for This Quiz:
_____Points

PHARISEES

You probably already know that the
Pharisees—the religious leaders of the day—
had an ongoing battle with Jesus. Can you
remember specifics of their conflict?

Answers on next page.

100

What civic duty did the Pharisees hope to use to
get Jesus in trouble with Caesar?

200

What short word, meaning "trouble," did Jesus
pronounce on the Pharisees seven times in one
speech?

300

What did Jesus do on a Sabbath day that so
infuriated the Pharisees they began plotting to
kill Him?

400

What type of person did Jesus use to contrast
with the self-righteous Pharisees in a parable on
humility?

500

What did Jesus say the Pharisees would see
in response to their demand for a sign from
heaven?

PHARISEES ANSWERS

100
paying taxes (Luke 20:20–26)

200
woe (Matthew 23:13–32)

300
heal (Matthew 12:9–14)

400
a tax collector, or publican (Luke 18:9–14)

500
the sign of Jonah (Matthew 16:1–4)

Your Score for This Quiz:
_____Points

Cumulative Score, P Quizzes:
_____Points

PONTIUS PILATE

The perfect politician—Pilate said he could find no fault in Jesus, but allowed Him to be crucified anyway. What else do you know about this Roman official?

Answers on next page.

100
What symbolic act did Pontius Pilate perform to try to brush aside responsibility for Jesus' crucifixion?

200
What position of authority did Pontius Pilate hold?

300
Who urged Pontius Pilate to leave Jesus alone after having a dream about Him?

400
What three-word question did Pontius Pilate utter after Jesus said He had come into the world to testify to the truth?

500
What fellow government official—formerly an enemy—became Pontius Pilate's friend during Jesus' trial?

PONTIUS PILATE ANSWERS

100
He washed his hands (Matthew 27:24)

200
governor (Matthew 27:2)

300
Pilate's wife (Matthew 27:19)

400
"What is truth?" (John 18:37–38)

500
Herod (Luke 23:5–12)

Your Score for This Quiz:
_____Points

Cumulative Score, P Quizzes:
_____Points

PROFIT AND LOSS

You don't have to be an accountant to understand the Bible's system of profit and loss. Can you add to your score by answering these five questions?

Answers on next page.

100
What did the apostle Paul say is profitable, or useful, for teaching, rebuking, correcting, and training in righteousness?

200
What did Jesus say a man could forfeit, negating the gain of "the whole world"?

300
What, along with godliness, did the apostle Paul tell Timothy "is great gain"?

400
Whose loss, according to the book of Romans, meant "riches" for the Gentiles?

500
How did Paul describe everything he had lost in his life in his efforts to gain Christ?

PROFIT AND LOSS ANSWERS

100
scripture (2 Timothy 3:16)

200
his soul (Mark 8:36)

300
contentment (1 Timothy 6:6)

400
Israel (Romans 11:7–12)

500
garbage, or dung (Philippians 3:7–8)

Your Score for This Quiz:
_____Points

Cumulative Score, P Quizzes:
_____Points

RISK IT!

Psalms

Congratulations—you've reached the *Risk It!* section for the *P* quizzes. Feel confident on the Psalms? Decide how much of your total score on the *P* quizzes you want to risk on the one question to follow. If you answer correctly, you add the amount you risked to your total *P* quiz score . . .if you answer incorrectly, you *subtract* the amount you risked. Made your decision? Write down the amount you're willing to risk, and we'll unveil the question. . . .

Your Total Score, P Quizzes:
_____Points

Your Risk It! Amount:
_____ Points

What did the psalmist say God's words, or promises, are sweeter than?

Answer on next page.

RISK IT! ANSWER

honey (Psalm 119:103)

Your Total Score, P Quizzes:
_____Points

+ or – Your Risk It! Amount:
_____Points

Running Total (A through P Quizzes):
_____Points

"Q" IT UP

There aren't a lot of "*Q* words" in the
Bible. . .but there are enough to fill
this category. What's your Bible IQ?

Answers on next page.

100

What ruler of Sheba, intrigued by reports of
Solomon's wisdom, paid a visit to test Solomon
with hard questions?

200

What arrow-carrying case did the psalmist liken
to a man with many sons?

300

What kind of bird did God miraculously provide
for the Israelites, who had grown tired of
manna?

400

What adjective, besides "peaceful," describes
the kind of Christian life Paul told Timothy to
live?

500

How did Jesus instruct Judas Iscariot to do his
evil work of betrayal?

"Q" IT UP ANSWERS

100
queen (1 Kings 10:1)

200
quiver (Psalm 127:4–5)

300
quail (Numbers 11:31–32)

400
quiet (1 Timothy 2:1–2)

500
quickly (John 13:27)

Your Score for This Quiz:
_____Points

QUENCHING

You don't often hear the word "quench"
used in everyday speech. . .but it's
a prominent word in the Bible.
Tell us what you know about it.

Answers on next page.

100
What terrible locale, according to Jesus, is a
place where "the fire is not quenched"?

200
What did the apostle Paul warn the
Thessalonians against quenching—or putting out
its fire?

300
What piece of the armor of God can quench the
fiery darts or flaming arrows of Satan?

400
What, according to the Song of Songs, cannot
quench love?

500
What captain in Deborah's army is listed in
Hebrews as a hero of faith, among those who
"quenched the fury of the flames"?

QUENCHING ANSWERS

100
hell (Mark 9:45–48)

200
the Spirit (1 Thessalonians 5:19)

300
the shield of faith (Ephesians 6:16)

400
many waters (Song of Songs 8:7)

500
Barak (Judges 4:14–15, Hebrews 11:32–34)

Your Score for This Quiz:
_____Points

Cumulative Score, Q Quizzes:
_____Points

QUESTIONS

Here are some questions about questions. But the real question is, "Do you have answers?"

Answers on next page.

100
Who did Jesus say He was calling to repentance when Pharisees asked why He ate with disreputable people?

200
What "visual aid" did Jesus use to answer the disciples' question, "Who is the greatest in the kingdom of heaven?"

300
What imprisoned preacher sent his own disciples to Jesus to ask if He was the expected Messiah?

400
What answer did Jesus give to an expert in the law who asked which commandment was greatest?

500
What two-part answer did Jesus give to troublemaking Pharisees who asked Him whether they should pay taxes to Caesar?

QUESTIONS ANSWERS

100
sinners (Matthew 9:10–13)

200
a child (Matthew 18:1–4)

300
John the Baptist (Matthew 11:1–15)

400
"Love the Lord your God with all your heart and with all your soul and with all your mind" (Matthew 22:34–40)

500
"Give to Caesar what is Caesar's and to God what is God's" (Mark 12:13–17)

Your Score for This Quiz:
_____Points

Cumulative Score, Q Quizzes:
_____Points

QUICKLY!

This is a quiz about the quick.
What do you know about Bible
characters and things that go fast?

Answers on next page.

100

Which disciple, according to Luke, ran to Jesus' tomb after faithful women told him of the Lord's resurrection?

200

What phrases describe the time frame in which Christians will be changed at the sound of the last trumpet?

300

What prostitute urged the men of Jericho to quickly pursue two Israelite spies—while she harbored those spies in her own home?

400

What prophet summoned fire from heaven to destroy fifty-one soldiers carrying King Ahaziah's command to "Come down at once!"?

500

What king of Israel was known for his furious chariot driving—likened to the driving of "a maniac"?

QUICKLY! ANSWERS

100
Peter (Luke 24:1–12)

200
"in a flash, in the twinkling of an eye"
(1 Corinthians 15:52)

300
Rahab (Joshua 2:1–6)

400
Elijah (2 Kings 1:1–12)

500
Jehu (2 Kings 9:2–3, 20)

Your Score for This Quiz:
_____Points

Cumulative Score, Q Quizzes:
_____Points

RISK IT!

Quarrelsome People

The *Q* questions are history. . .now it's
time to *Risk It!* What do you know about
quarrelsome people in the Bible? Choose
how much of your total score on the *Q*
quizzes you want to risk on the one question
following. If you answer correctly, you
add the amount you risked to your total *Q*
quiz score. . .if you answer incorrectly, you
subtract the amount you risked. Made up your
mind yet? Note the amount you're willing
to risk, and we'll unveil the question. . . .

Your Total Score, Q Quizzes:
_____Points

Your Risk It! Amount:
_____ Points

Where did Moses obtain water for the quarreling
Israelites at a dry place called Kadesh?

Answer on next page.

RISK IT! ANSWER

from a rock (Numbers 20:1–11)

Your Total Score, Q Quizzes:
_____Points

+ or – Your Risk It! Amount:
_____Points

Running Total (A through Q Quizzes):
_____Points

RICHES OF EARTH

No, this isn't a quiz about guys named Rich. We're talking money, moolah, dinero. . .and what the Bible says about it. Put your money where your mouth is, and tell us what you know.

Answers on next page.

100
What feeling toward money is "a root of all kinds of evil"?

200
What two things, according to Jesus, destroy treasures on earth?

300
What coming day, according to the Proverbs, shows the worthlessness of wealth?

400
What dishonest quality of wealth, according to Jesus' parable of the sower, causes some Christians to be unfruitful?

500
What word did the apostle Paul use to describe wealth or riches in his first letter to Timothy?

RICHES OF EARTH ANSWERS

100
love (1 Timothy 6:10)

200
moth and vermin, or rust (Matthew 6:19)

300
the day of wrath (Proverbs 11:4)

400
deceitfulness (Matthew 13:22)

500
uncertain (1 Timothy 6:17)

Your Score for This Quiz:
_____Points

RIVERS

You won't find the Mississippi or the Amazon in the Bible, but several other rivers are noted. What do you recall of them?

Answers on next page.

100
What future leader of Israel, as a three-month-old baby, was placed in a basket in the river of Egypt—the Nile?

200
What form did the Holy Spirit take when it descended on Jesus after His baptism in the Jordan River?

300
Of the four rivers that were said to flow from the Garden of Eden, what two share names with important rivers of the modern Middle East?

400
What leprous army commander, told to wash in the Jordan for healing, preferred to wash in the Abana or Pharpar rivers of his homeland?

500
Where does "the river of the water of life" in the new Jerusalem originate?

RIVERS ANSWERS

100
Moses (Exodus 2:1–10)

200
a dove (Matthew 3:13–17)

300
Tigris and Euphrates (Genesis 2:10–14)

400
Naaman (2 Kings 5:10–14)

500
the throne of God (Revelation 22:1–2)

Your Score for This Quiz:
_____Points

Cumulative Score, R Quizzes:
_____Points

RUTH'S STORY

Looking for a little romance? Try the
Bible's story of Ruth—that's where
the questions in this quiz come from.

Answers on next page.

100
What great-grandson of Ruth became the most
prominent king of Israel?

200
What was Ruth doing the first time she saw
Boaz, the man she would marry?

300
What role did Boaz play by marrying Ruth and
purchasing the property of her former in-laws?

400
What was the name of Ruth's first husband, who
died?

500
What name, meaning "Bitter," did Ruth's newly-
widowed mother-in-law give herself?

RUTH'S STORY ANSWERS

100
David (Ruth 4:13–17)

200
gleaning (Ruth 2:5–8)

300
guardian-, or kinsman-redeemer (Ruth 3:7–13)

400
Mahlon (Ruth 4:10)

500
Mara (Ruth 1:20)

Your Score for This Quiz:
_____Points

Cumulative Score, R Quizzes:
_____Points

"R" YOU SURE?

You noticed the quotation marks?
Then you already know that every answer
in this quiz begins with the letter *R*.

Answers on next page.

100
What did Jesus say He came to call sinners to?

200
What daughter of Bethuel was wife of the patriarch Isaac?

300
What kind of lion does the apostle Peter compare the devil to?

400
What name—also the name of a bay in Delaware—did Isaac give to a well he dug?

500
What kind of fire does the prophet Malachi say the Lord will be like in the day of judgment?

"R" YOU SURE? ANSWERS

100
repentance (Luke 5:31–32)

200
Rebekah (Genesis 25:20)

300
roaring (1 Peter 5:8)

400
Rehoboth (Genesis 26:22)

500
refiner's (Malachi 3:1–2)

Your Score for This Quiz:
_____Points

Cumulative Score, R Quizzes:
_____Points

RISK IT!

Revenge

And now you can *Risk It!* for the four *R* quizzes—as we test your knowledge of the category "Revenge." Consider how much of your total score on the *R* quizzes you want to risk on the one question to follow. If you answer correctly, you add the amount you risked to your total *R* quiz score. . .if you answer incorrectly, you *subtract* the amount you risked. Settled on a number? Write down the amount you're willing to risk, and we'll unveil the question. . . .

Your Total Score, R Quizzes:
_____Points

Your Risk It! Amount:
_____ Points

What three words complete God's promise, "It is mine to avenge; . . ." quoted by Paul in his letter to the Romans?

Answer on next page.

RISK IT! ANSWER

"I will repay" (Romans 12:19)

Your Total Score, R Quizzes:
_____Points

+ or – Your Risk It! Amount:
_____Points

Running Total (A through R Quizzes):
_____Points

SALT

Salt—chemical compound NaCl—was pretty important stuff in the Bible. Tell us what you know about salt, both literal and figurative.

Answers on next page.

100
Whose wife was turned into a pillar of salt for looking back on the doomed cities of Sodom and Gomorrah?

200
What did Jesus tell His disciples they were "the salt of"?

300
What did the apostle Paul say should be "seasoned with salt"?

400
What did Mark quote Jesus as saying everyone would be "salted with"?

500
What Old Testament prophet healed the waters of Jericho by throwing salt into a spring?

SALT ANSWERS

100
Lot (Genesis 19:23–26)

200
the earth (Matthew 5:13)

300
conversation, or speech (Colossians 4:6)

400
fire (Mark 9:49)

500
Elisha (2 Kings 2:19–22)

Your Score for This Quiz:
_____Points

SIMON WHO?

Simon was a popular name in Bible times. Here are five men who were known by the name Simon—your job is to more clearly identify each one.

Answers on next page.

100
What did a Simon from Cyrene carry for Jesus as He walked to His execution?

200
What famous half-brother could a certain Simon, with his full brothers James, Joseph, and Judas, claim?

300
What two-word nickname—from a dreaded disease he had—described a Simon from Bethany?

400
What forbidden art did a Simon from Samaria practice before he accepted Christ?

500
What job was held by a Simon from Joppa, who entertained the apostle Peter in his house by the sea?

SIMON WHO? ANSWERS

100
His cross (Luke 23:26)

200
Jesus (Matthew 13:53–56)

300
"the Leper" (Mark 14:3)

400
sorcery (Acts 8:9–24)

500
tanner (Acts 10:30–33)

Your Score for This Quiz:
_____Points

Cumulative Score, S Quizzes:
_____Points

"S"ONS OF MEN

Two hints on this quiz: Every answer
begins with the letter S, and each
answer is the name of a biblical man.

Answers on next page.

100

What man is generally listed first in the accounts
of Noah's sons?

200

What man, described in Acts as "full of faith and
of the Holy Spirit," was one of seven chosen to
relieve the apostles of waiting on tables?

300

What devout man held the baby Jesus when
Mary and Joseph presented Him at the temple?

400

What king of Assyria insulted God to King
Hezekiah of Judah—and paid for it with his life?

500

What man, a Horonite, opposed Nehemiah and
the Jews rebuilding the walls of Jerusalem?

"S"ONS OF MEN ANSWERS

100
Shem (Genesis 5:32)

200
Stephen (Acts 6:1–5)

300
Simeon (Luke 2:25–32)

400
Sennacherib (2 Kings 19:5–13, 35–37)

500
Sanballat (Nehemiah 2:10, 4:1–2)

Your Score for This Quiz:
_____Points

Cumulative Score, S Quizzes:
_____Points

SOUL WINNERS

Call it "evangelism," "preaching the gospel," or "bringing in the sheaves." Christians have an obligation to win souls. What do you recall about the Bible's soul-winning passages?

Answers on next page.

100

What two disciples from Jesus' inner circle, described as "unschooled, ordinary men," amazed the Jewish leaders with their courage in preaching the gospel?

200

What agricultural term did Jesus use to describe the soul-winners' goal?

300

What businesswoman from Thyatira, a seller of purple cloth, became a Christian after hearing Paul share the gospel?

400

What word did Solomon, in the Proverbs, use to describe soul winners?

500

What five-word phrase did the apostle Paul say he had become in his efforts to bring various people to Christ?

SOUL WINNERS ANSWERS

100
Peter and John (Acts 4:1–20)

200
harvest (Luke 10:1–2)

300
Lydia (Acts 16:13–15)

400
wise (Proverbs 11:30)

500
"all things to all people," or "men"
(1 Corinthians 9:22)

Your Score for This Quiz:
_____Points

Cumulative Score, S Quizzes:
_____Points

RISK IT!

Satan's Schemes

Well, you've gone through all four S quizzes and reached the *Risk It!* portion of the game. Let's test your knowledge of Satan's schemes in the Bible. Think over how much of your total score on the S quizzes you want to risk on the one question following. If you answer correctly, you add the amount you risked to your total S quiz score . . .if you answer incorrectly, you *subtract* the amount you risked. Have you decided? Mark down the amount you're willing to risk, and we'll unveil the question. . . .

Your Total Score, S Quizzes:
_____Points

Your Risk It! Amount:
_____ Points

How many days had Jesus fasted in the desert when Satan tempted Him to turn stones into bread?

Answer on next page.

RISK IT! ANSWER

forty (Matthew 4:1–4)

Your Total Score, S Quizzes:
_____Points

+ or – Your Risk It! Amount:
_____Points

Running Total (A through S Quizzes):
_____Points

TITHES AND OFFERINGS

The apostle Paul quoted Jesus as saying,
"It is more blessed to give than to receive."
What do you know about the Bible's
instruction on tithes and offerings?

Answers on next page.

100
What attitude of giving, according to the apostle
Paul, does God love?

200
Which day of the week did the apostle Paul tell
believers to put aside money for their offerings?

300
What two words describe the woman Jesus
commended for giving an offering of two small
copper coins—or "mites"?

400
What priest of Salem received a tithe from the
patriarch Abram, later called Abraham?

500
What three spices did Jesus scold Pharisees for
tithing while neglecting more important issues
like justice and mercy?

TITHES AND OFFERINGS ANSWERS

100
cheerful (2 Corinthians 9:7)

200
the first day (1 Corinthians 16:2)

300
"poor widow" (Mark 12:41–43)

400
Melchizedek (Genesis 14:18–20)

500
mint, dill (or anise), and cumin (Matthew 23:23)

Your Score for This Quiz:
_____Points

TOMBS

Yeah, we're talking about tombs—those places that hold dead bodies. You'll find quite a few of them in Scripture. . . . What do you remember about these?

Answers on next page.

100
Whose tomb was marked by a pillar erected by her husband, Jacob?

200
What kind of tomb did Jesus derisively use to describe the hypocritical Pharisees and teachers of the law?

300
Who gave up his own new tomb for the burial of the crucified Jesus?

400
What Old Testament woman was buried in a cave in the field of Machpelah?

500
What son and grandson of Kish were reburied in his tomb after their deaths in battle?

TOMBS ANSWERS

100
Rachel (Genesis 35:19–20)

200
whitewashed, or whited (Matthew 23:27–28)

300
Joseph of Arimathea (Matthew 27:57–60)

400
Sarah (Genesis 23:19)

500
Saul and Jonathan (2 Samuel 21:13–14)

Your Score for This Quiz:
_____Points

Cumulative Score, T Quizzes:
_____Points

TREES

They didn't have Arbor Day, but they did have plenty of trees. Show us your knowledge of these trees of the Bible.

Answers on next page.

100
What kind of tree did a man named Zacchaeus climb in order to see Jesus?

200
What type of tree immediately withered when Jesus cursed it—an event Jesus used to teach His disciples about faith?

300
What famous tree of Lebanon was used by the psalmist as a metaphor for the righteous?

400
What kind of tree was Gideon working under when the angel of the Lord greeted him?

500
What type of tree does the love-smitten woman of the Song of Songs compare her man to?

TREES ANSWERS

100
sycamore-fig (Luke 19:1–4)

200
fig (Matthew 21:18–22)

300
cedar (Psalm 92:12)

400
oak (Judges 6:11–12)

500
apple (Song of Songs 2:3)

Your Score for This Quiz:
_____Points

Cumulative Score, T Quizzes:
_____Points

"T" TIME

Another set of quotation marks, and another tip-off to aid you: All of the following answers will begin with the letter *T*.

Answers on next page.

100
What troublesome desire did Paul say is "common to mankind"?

200
What city was the birthplace of the apostle Paul?

300
Where did Abraham find a ram to sacrifice after God stopped him from sacrificing his son Isaac?

400
What two *T*s grew from the ground God cursed after Adam and Eve's sin?

500
Which of the churches of Revelation did Jesus criticize for tolerating "that woman Jezebel"?

"T" TIME ANSWERS

100
temptation (1 Corinthians 10:13)

200
Tarsus (Acts 22:2–3)

300
thicket (Genesis 22:9–13)

400
thorns and thistles (Genesis 3:17–18)

500
Thyatira (Revelation 2:18–20)

Your Score for This Quiz:
_____Points

Cumulative Score, T Quizzes:
_____Points

RISK IT!

Thomas

It's time to *Risk It!* for the *T* quizzes. What do you know about Thomas? Think about how much of your total score on the *T* quizzes you want to risk on the one question following. If you answer correctly, you add the amount you risked to your total *T* quiz score. . .if you answer incorrectly, you *subtract* the amount you risked. Got your number? Mark down the amount you're willing to risk, and we'll unveil the question. . . .

Your Total Score, T Quizzes:
_____Points

Your Risk It! Amount:
_____ Points

What second name was Thomas known by?

Answer on next page.

RISK IT! ANSWER

Didymus (John 11:16)

Your Total Score, T Quizzes:
_____Points

+ or – Your Risk It! Amount:
_____Points

Running Total (A through T Quizzes):
_____Points

"U" KNOW?

We've called out the letter *U* in the title to this quiz. That lets you know the first letter of each answer.

Answers on next page.

100
In what kind of room did Jesus celebrate His last Passover with His disciples?

200
What, along with wisdom, does Solomon urge readers of the Proverbs to get?

300
What land did the patriarch Abraham hail from?

400
What kind of god had the people of Athens built an altar to—prompting the apostle Paul to share the true God with them?

500
What man, attempting to steady the ark of the covenant on its cart, was struck dead for touching it?

"U" KNOW? ANSWERS

100
upstairs, or upper (Mark 14:12–15)

200
understanding (Proverbs 4:5–7)

300
Ur of the Chaldeans (Genesis 15:7–8)

400
unknown (Acts 17:22–23)

500
Uzzah (2 Samuel 6:6–7)

Your Score for This Quiz:
_____Points

UNTO US A CHILD IS BORN

The birth of Christ—a remarkable fulfillment of prophecy and a key event in all human history. What do you remember of the Bible's Christmas story?

Answers on next page.

100
What town in Judea was the birthplace of Jesus?

200
What animal feeding trough served as a temporary bed for the newborn Jesus?

300
What name, meaning "God with us," did Isaiah prophesy for Jesus?

400
What relative did Jesus' mother, Mary, stay with while she was expecting?

500
What, according to the prophet Isaiah, would Jesus carry on His shoulders?

UNTO US A CHILD IS BORN ANSWERS

100
Bethlehem (Matthew 2:1)

200
a manger (Luke 2:7)

300
Immanuel or Emmanuel (Isaiah 7:14,
Matthew 1:22–23)

400
Elizabeth (Luke 1:36, 56)

500
the government (Isaiah 9:6)

Your Score for This Quiz:
_____Points

Cumulative Score, U Quizzes:
_____Points

UPROARS

Call 'em riots, hubbubs, or donnybrooks,
you'll find a number of uproars in
the pages of scripture! What can
you tell us about these?

Answers on next page.

100
What idol were the Israelites worshiping with
shouting and singing when Moses arrived with
God's Ten Commandments?

200
What disciple was martyred by an angry,
screaming crowd, after a critical speech to the
Sanhedrin?

300
What did Moses fear the thirsty Israelites would
do to him at a dry place called Rephidim?

400
In what city did silversmiths—fearing the
effect of Paul's preaching on their idol-making
business—stir up a riot?

500
What two groups of people, according to
the crowd at Jesus' crucifixion, should bear
responsibility for Jesus' death?

UPROARS ANSWERS

100
the golden calf (Exodus 32:1–4, 17–20)

200
Stephen (Acts 7:51–60)

300
stone him (Exodus 17:1–4)

400
Ephesus (Acts 19:25–32)

500
"us and. . .our children" (Matthew 27:25)

Your Score for This Quiz:
_____Points

Cumulative Score, U Quizzes:
_____Points

URIAH THE HITTITE

He had a beautiful wife—and that got him killed. What else do you recall of the story of Uriah the Hittite?

Answers on next page.

100

What beautiful wife of Uriah was improperly taken—and made pregnant—by a lustful King David?

200

What was Uriah's occupation?

300

How many nights did David try to make Uriah go home to sleep with his wife?

400

Where did King David later order Uriah?

500

What prophet confronted David about his sins toward Uriah?

URIAH THE HITTITE ANSWERS

100
Bathsheba (2 Samuel 11:2–5)

200
soldier (2 Samuel 11:7)

300
two (2 Samuel 11:8–13)

400
the fiercest part of the battle, to his death
(2 Samuel 11:14–15)

500
Nathan (2 Samuel 12:1–10)

Your Score for This Quiz:
_____Points

Cumulative Score, U Quizzes:
_____Points

RISK IT!

Unclean! Unclean!

It's time to *Risk It!* for the *U* quizzes.
What do you know about those dramatic
words, "Unclean! Unclean!"? Think about
how much of your total score on the *U*
quizzes you want to risk on the one question
following. If you answer correctly, you add
the amount you risked to your total *U* quiz
score. . .if you answer incorrectly, you *subtract*
the amount you risked. Got your number?
Mark down the amount you're willing to risk,
and we'll unveil the question. . . .

Your Total Score, U Quizzes:
_____Points

Your Risk It! Amount:
_____ Points

How many leprous men came to Jesus
requesting a mass healing—for which only one
returned to praise God?

Answer on next page.

RISK IT! ANSWER

ten (Luke 17:11–19)

Your Total Score, U Quizzes:
_____Points

+ or – Your Risk It! Amount:
_____Points

Running Total (A through U Quizzes):
_____Points

VICTORY AND DEFEAT

You win some, you lose some. . . . *You* could
be a winner, depending on how much you
know about biblical victories and defeats.

Answers on next page.

100
What weapon did the young David use to fell the
giant warrior Goliath?

200
What hostile army, pursuing the people of Israel,
was completely destroyed in the middle of the
Red Sea?

300
What, according to 1 Corinthians, will be
"swallowed up in victory" at the last trumpet?

400
What three-word phrase did Paul use to describe
believers who may suffer persecution, famine,
and danger—but who are never separated from
the love of Christ?

500
What miracle occurred in the heavens the day
Joshua and the Israelites defeated the armies of
the five kings of the Amorites?

VICTORY AND DEFEAT ANSWERS

100
a sling (1 Samuel 17:4, 50)

200
the Egyptians (Exodus 14:21–28)

300
death (1 Corinthians 15:51–54)

400
"more than conquerors" (Romans 8:35–39)

500
the sun stood still (Joshua 10:9–14)

Your Score for This Quiz:
_____Points

VIPERS

No, not the sports car by Dodge. . .
we're talking about the slithering,
sneaky, snaky kind of viper. Do you
remember these stories?

Answers on next page.

100
What religious group did Jesus twice call a
"brood (or generation) of vipers"?

200
What Egyptian leader disregarded Moses and
Aaron's miracle of turning a staff into a snake?

300
What forbidden tree in the Garden of Eden did
the serpent convince Eve to eat from?

400
What metal did Moses use to fashion a snake
image that healed Israelites bitten by venomous
serpents?

500
What sparkling substance does the writer of
Proverbs compare to the poison of a viper?

VIPERS ANSWERS

100
the Pharisees (Matthew 12:24–34, 23:29–33)

200
Pharaoh (Exodus 7:10–13)

300
the tree of the knowledge of good and evil
(Genesis 2:15–17, 3:1–6)

400
bronze, or brass (Numbers 21:4–9)

500
wine (Proverbs 23:31–32)

Your Score for This Quiz:
_____Points

Cumulative Score, V Quizzes:
_____Points

VISIONS

Visions appear throughout the Bible—
both Old Testament and New. Can
you recall details of these five?

Answers on next page.

100
What suffering Old Testament saint complained that God would "terrify" him with visions?

200
What apostle had a vision of animals being let down from heaven in a sheet—and realized God had offered salvation to the Gentiles?

300
What Israelite leader did God speak with face-to-face rather than in visions?

400
How many golden lamp stands, each representing a church in Asia Minor, did John see in his vision of the Revelation of Christ?

500
What two animals appeared in a prophetic vision of Daniel's, near the Ulai Canal?

VISIONS ANSWERS

100
Job (Job 7:13–14)

200
Peter (Acts 11:1–18)

300
Moses (Numbers 12:6–8)

400
seven (Revelation 1:12–20)

500
ram and goat (Daniel 8:1–12)

Your Score for This Quiz:
_____Points

Cumulative Score, V Quizzes:
_____Points

VOICE OF GOD

When God speaks, you'd better listen!
Were you paying attention when God
spoke in these Bible passages?

Answers on next page.

100
What storm-related phenomenon is likened to
God's voice in the books of Job and John?

200
Where was the persecutor Saul going when he
was stopped on the road and converted by the
voice of Jesus?

300
What excuse did Adam give for hiding when he
heard God's voice?

400
What two Old Testament figures appeared at
Jesus' transfiguration, when God's voice was
heard saying, "This is my Son, whom I love; with
him I am well pleased"?

500
What three-word title, later applied to Jesus
Christ, did the voice of God use to address the
prophet Ezekiel?

VOICE OF GOD ANSWERS

100
thunder (Job 37:4–5; John 12:23–29)

200
Damascus (Acts 9:1–6)

300
afraid, naked (either answer acceptable)
(Genesis 3:9–10)

400
Moses and Elijah (Matthew 17:1–5)

500
"son of man" (Ezekiel 2:1; Matthew 8:20)

Your Score for This Quiz:
_____Points

Cumulative Score, V Quizzes:
_____Points

RISK IT!

Vows

All right. . .you've completed the *V* quizzes, and it's time to *Risk It!* How confident are you on the category "Vows"? Consider how much of your total score on the *V* quizzes you want to risk on the one question following. If you answer correctly, you add the amount you risked to your total *V* quiz score. . .if you answer incorrectly, you *subtract* the amount you risked. Are you ready? Write down the amount you're willing to risk, and we'll unveil the question. . . .

Your Total Score, V Quizzes:
_____Points

Your Risk It! Amount:
_____ Points

What judge of Israel made a foolish vow that cost him the life of his only daughter?

Answer on next page.

RISK IT! ANSWER

Jephthah (Judges 11:30–39)

Your Total Score, V Quizzes:
_____Points

+ or – Your Risk It! Amount:
_____Points

Running Total (A through V Quizzes):
_____Points

WISDOM

It seems in short supply in today's world, but the Bible is packed with words of wisdom. How wise will you be when it comes to these questions?

Answers on next page.

100
What precious metal, according to Proverbs, cannot compare to the value of wisdom?

200
What does Proverbs say is the "beginning of wisdom"?

300
To whom, according to Proverbs, does a man who loves wisdom bring joy?

400
What relative do the Proverbs say a young man should call wisdom?

500
According to Proverbs, what does the person who gets wisdom love?

WISDOM ANSWERS

100
gold (Proverbs 16:16)

200
the fear of the LORD (Proverbs 9:10)

300
his father (Proverbs 29:3)

400
sister (Proverbs 7:4)

500
life, or his own soul (Proverbs 19:8)

Your Score for This Quiz:
_____Points

WIVES

Wives in the Bible come in all varieties—good, bad, and indifferent. What can you recall about these?

Answers on next page.

100
What great patriarch took a wife named Keturah after his first wife died?

200
How many wives did Solomon have—in addition to his three hundred concubines?

300
What daughter of King Saul became the wife of David—for the price of two hundred dead Philistines?

400
Which apostle's wife accompanied him on ministry trips, according to Paul?

500
What second wife of Elkanah provoked his other wife, Hannah, over her barrenness?

WIVES ANSWERS

100
Abraham (Genesis 25:1)

200
seven hundred (1 Kings 11:1–3)

300
Michal (1 Samuel 18:26–27)

400
Peter, or Cephas (1 Corinthians 9:5)

500
Peninnah (1 Samuel 1:1–6)

Your Score for This Quiz:
_____Points

Cumulative Score, W Quizzes:
_____Points

"W"ORDS OF THE BIBLE

Here's your big hint—because you see quotation marks in the quiz title, all of the answers will begin with the letter *W*.

Answers on next page.

100
What did God use to take the prophet Elijah into heaven?

200
What word is paired with "signs" to describe the miraculous doings of the apostles after Pentecost?

300
What ravenous animal would feed peacefully with the lamb in the new earth prophesied by Isaiah?

400
What did the patriarch Jacob do all night with God at a place called Peniel?

500
What is the name of the star that falls to earth and poisons a third of the water, as described in Revelation?

"W"ORDS OF THE BIBLE ANSWERS

100
whirlwind (2 Kings 2:1)

200
wonders (Acts 5:12)

300
wolf (Isaiah 65:25)

400
wrestle (Genesis 32:22–30)

500
Wormwood (Revelation 8:10–11)

Your Score for This Quiz:
_____Points

Cumulative Score, W Quizzes:
_____Points

WORKERS

You've worked your way through most
of the alphabet, to a quiz about "workers."
Give your memory a good workout
and try to answer these questions.

Answers on next page.

100
What word did Jesus use to describe the workers
compared to the "plentiful" harvest of souls?

200
What did the apostle Paul, writing to the
Thessalonians, say that those who refused to
work should be kept from doing?

300
What man, who once deserted Paul's mission
work in Pamphylia, did the apostle later call
"helpful" and ask Timothy to bring to him?

400
What did Jesus once say a worker was worthy of?

500
What word did the writer of Ecclesiastes use to
describe the sleep of a laborer?

WORKERS ANSWERS

100
few (Luke 10:2)

200
eating (2 Thessalonians 3:10)

300
(John) Mark (Acts 15:37–38, 2 Timothy 4:11)

400
his wages, or hire (Luke 10:7)

500
sweet (Ecclesiastes 5:12)

Your Score for This Quiz:
_____Points

Cumulative Score, W Quizzes:
_____Points

RISK IT!

Write a Letter

Here we are at the *Risk It!* category for the four *W* quizzes. Let's test your knowledge in the category "Write a Letter." Decide how much of your total score on the *W* quizzes you want to risk on the one question following. If you answer correctly, you add the amount you risked to your total *W* quiz score. . .if you answer incorrectly, you *subtract* the amount you risked. Have a figure in mind? Mark down the amount you're willing to risk, and we'll unveil the question. . . .

Your Total Score, W Quizzes:
_____Points

Your Risk It! Amount:
_____ Points

What special prisoner was the subject of a letter from Claudius Lysias to Governor Felix?

Answer on next page.

RISK IT! ANSWER

the apostle Paul (Acts 23:25–31)

Your Total Score, W Quizzes:
_____Points

+ or – Your Risk It! Amount:
_____Points

Running Total (A through W Quizzes):
_____Points

X AT THE END

Words starting with *X* are relatively uncommon. . .but it's not unusual to find words *ending* with *X*. Don't worry, you can handle this quiz—relax!

Answers on next page.

100
What did Jesus and Peter pay with a coin found in a fish's mouth?

200
What animal were the Israelites not to muzzle as it was treading grain?

300
What melting substance did the psalmist say his heart had turned to?

400
What metal tool miraculously floated for the prophet Elisha?

500
What Egyptian crop was destroyed by the plague of hail called down by Moses?

X AT THE END ANSWERS

100
tax (Matthew 17:24–27)

200
ox (Deuteronomy 25:4)

300
wax (Psalm 22:14)

400
ax (2 Kings 6:1–7)

500
flax (Exodus 9:29–31)

Your Score for This Quiz:
_____Points

XENOPHOBIA

According to the dictionary, *xenophobia* is a fear and hatred of foreigners—and something God sometimes encouraged to keep His chosen people pure. What do you know about these five cases?

Answers on next page.

100
What did the patriarch Isaac forbid his son Jacob to do with a Canaanite woman?

200
What annual ritual dinner of the Israelites were foreigners forbidden to eat?

300
What charge for borrowed money could Israelites apply to foreigners but not to fellow Jews?

400
What nationality, hated by the Jews, provided the "good guy" character in Jesus' parable of a man beaten by robbers?

500
What type of agreement did God forbid between Israel and the nations He would drive out of the Promised Land?

XENOPHOBIA ANSWERS

100
marry (Genesis 28:1)

200
Passover (Exodus 12:43)

300
interest, or usury (Deuteronomy 23:19–20)

400
Samaritan (Luke 10:25–37)

500
treaty, or covenant (Deuteronomy 7:1–2)

Your Score for This Quiz:
_____Points

Cumulative Score, X Quizzes:
_____Points

XERXES

He's also known as Ahasuerus. . .
which is probably a good reason
to go by "Xerxes." Tell us what you
know about this ancient king.

Answers on next page.

100
What beautiful young Jewish woman was the
second queen of the Persian King Xerxes?

200
What modern-day nation, with its capital at
New Delhi, marked the eastern extent of King
Xerxes's nation?

300
Who discovered and foiled a plot to assassinate
King Xerxes?

400
What would King Xerxes hold out to show favor
to the people who pleased him?

500
What city was the site of King Xerxes's royal
citadel?

XERXES ANSWERS

100
Esther (Esther 2:16–17)

200
India (Esther 8:9)

300
Mordecai (Esther 2:21–23)

400
a golden scepter (Esther 4:11, 5:2)

500
Susa, or Shushan (Esther 1:2)

Your Score for This Quiz:
_____Points

Cumulative Score, X Quizzes:
_____Points

X-RAY VISION

Seeing through brick walls is a talent of the fictional Superman. But seeing through the walls of the heart is a power of the true God. What do you know about His "X-Ray Vision"?

Answers on next page.

100
What son did King David tell, "The LORD searches every heart and understands every desire and every thought"?

200
What troublemaking religious leaders—accusing Jesus of casting out demons by the prince of demons—had their thoughts read by Jesus?

300
What great prophet heard God say, "Man looks at the outward appearance, but the LORD looks at the heart"?

400
What did Jesus say God would do for the believers He sees secretly giving to the needy?

500
What "el"oquent friend of Job proclaimed God's complete knowledge, saying, "There is no deep shadow. . .where evildoers can hide"?

X-RAY VISION ANSWERS

100
Solomon (1 Chronicles 28:2–10)

200
Pharisees (Matthew 12:22–28)

300
Samuel (1 Samuel 16:7)

400
reward them (Matthew 6:3–4)

500
Elihu (Job 34:1–22)

Your Score for This Quiz:
_____Points

Cumulative Score, X Quizzes:
_____Points

RISK IT!

X Marks the Spot

You've gotten through the *X* quizzes. . . and now you'll *Risk It!* How does this "X Marks the Spot" category sound to you? Think over how much of your total score on the *X* quizzes you want to risk on the one question following. If you answer correctly, you add the amount you risked to your total *X* quiz score. . .if you answer incorrectly, you *subtract* the amount you risked. Have a figure in mind? Mark down the amount you're willing to risk, and we'll unveil the question. . . .

Your Total Score, X Quizzes:
_____Points

Your Risk It! Amount:
_____ Points

In a parable describing the kingdom of heaven, where did Jesus say a man found a hidden treasure?

Answer on next page.

RISK IT! ANSWER

in a field (Matthew 13:44)

Your Total Score, X Quizzes:
_____Points

+ or – Your Risk It! Amount:
_____Points

Running Total (A through X Quizzes):
_____Points

YACHTSMAN

Okay, okay. . .you won't find the word *yacht* in any translation of the Bible. But we're using it as a synonym for boat and asking you to tell us about the sailors of scripture.

Answers on next page.

100
What wayward prophet was thrown overboard by pagan sailors frightened by a violent storm at sea?

200
What alliterative brothers were in a boat when Jesus called them to be His disciples?

300
What was Jesus doing in a boat immediately before calming a storm that terrified His disciples?

400
What wise and wealthy king, who built God's first temple, also built ships on the Red Sea?

500
What island's people welcomed the apostle Paul and 275 other people after their ship broke apart in the Adriatic Sea?

YACHTSMEN ANSWERS

100
Jonah (Jonah 1:13–15)

200
James and John (Matthew 4:21–22)

300
sleeping (Luke 8:22–25)

400
Solomon (1 Kings 9:26–28)

500
Malta, or Melita (Acts 27:37–28:2)

Your Score for This Quiz:
_____Points

YELLOW-BELLIES

That's an Old West term for "cowards"—
and there were a few of them in the Bible.
Tell us what you remember about these.

Answers on next page.

100
How many times during Jesus' arrest and trial
did Simon Peter deny he knew the Lord?

200
What did the terrified disciples think they were
seeing when Jesus walked across the water to
their boat?

300
What wicked queen threatened the life of the
prophet Elijah, causing him to pray to God that
he would die?

400
What conspiring son of King David caused his
father to flee for his life from Jerusalem?

500
What Israelite leader, preparing for battle
against the Midianites, saw twenty-two thousand
warriors—more than two-thirds of his army—
desert when given the chance?

YELLOW-BELLIES ANSWERS

100
three (Luke 22:54–62)

200
a ghost, or spirit (Matthew 14:22–27)

300
Jezebel (1 Kings 19:1–4)

400
Absalom (2 Samuel 15:13–37)

500
Gideon (Judges 7:1–3)

Your Score for This Quiz:
_____Points

Cumulative Score, Y Quizzes:
_____Points

YOKES

Ha ha. . .the yoke's on you! Yeah, we know that's a bad pun, but there are yokes in the Bible that belong on people, as well as animals. What can you recall about them?

Answers on next page.

100
How did Jesus describe the yoke He places on His followers?

200
What color of heifer—which had never worn a yoke—were Moses and Aaron instructed to sacrifice?

300
What kind of yoking did the apostle Paul warn the church at Corinth about?

400
What Old Testament prophet wore a wooden yoke as an object lesson?

500
What king, the son of Solomon, threatened to place his subjects under a heavy yoke—and caused many of the tribes of Israel to rebel?

YOKES ANSWERS

100
easy (Matthew 11:28–30)

200
red (Numbers 19:1–5)

300
with unbelievers, or unequal (2 Corinthians 6:14)

400
Jeremiah (Jeremiah 28:12–14)

500
Rehoboam (1 Kings 12:1–19)

Your Score for This Quiz:
_____Points

Cumulative Score, Y Quizzes:
_____Points

YOUNG PEOPLE

You have to be thirty-five to become president of the United States. But you can serve the Lord at any age. What do you know about these five young people of the Bible?

Answers on next page.

100
What instrument did the young David play to soothe the troubled spirit of King Saul?

200
What boy, destined to become a great prophet of Israel, ministered in the temple under the priest Eli?

300
How old was the boy Jesus when He amazed people in the temple with His spiritual insights?

400
What young king removed all the mediums and spiritists from Judah, as required in the book of the law found by his priest, Hilkiah?

500
What young relative of Paul discovered and reported a plot to kill the apostle in Jerusalem?

YOUNG PEOPLE ANSWERS

100
lyre, or harp (1 Samuel 16:18–23)

200
Samuel (1 Samuel 3:1)

300
twelve (Luke 2:41–52)

400
Josiah (2 Kings 22:1–8, 23:24–25)

500
his nephew, or sister's son (Acts 23:12–22)

Your Score for This Quiz:
_____Points

Cumulative Score, Y Quizzes:
_____Points

RISK IT!

Yearly Things

It's time again to *Risk It!*—this time, for your score on the four Y quizzes. We're talking about yearly things in the Bible. Decide how much of your total score on the Y quizzes you want to risk on the one question following. If you answer correctly, you add the amount you risked to your total Y quiz score. . .if you answer incorrectly, you *subtract* the amount you risked. Are you ready? Jot down the amount you're willing to risk, and we'll unveil the question. . . .

Your Total Score, Y Quizzes:
_____Points

Your Risk It! Amount:
_____ Points

What annual celebration was instituted to commemorate the Jews' victory over their enemies in Queen Esther's time?

Answer on next page.

RISK IT! ANSWER

Purim (Esther 9:20–28)

Your Total Score, Y Quizzes:
_____Points

+ or – Your Risk It! Amount:
_____Points

Running Total (A through Y Quizzes):
_____Points

ZACCHAEUS

If you know the Sunday school song about Zacchaeus, you might want to sing it to yourself. . . . It'll probably help you answer some of these questions!

Answers on next page.

100
What physical characteristic initially hindered Zacchaeus from seeing Jesus?

200
What was Zacchaeus's line of work?

300
What derogatory name did the crowd call Zacchaeus when Jesus visited his home?

400
What town was home to Zacchaeus?

500
How much did Zacchaeus promise to pay back to anyone he had cheated?

ZACCHAEUS ANSWERS

100
shortness (Luke 19:3)

200
tax collector, or publican (Luke 19:2)

300
"a sinner" (Luke 19:7)

400
Jericho (Luke 19:1, 5–6)

500
four times the amount (Luke 19:8)

Your Score for This Quiz:
_____Points

ZECHARIAH WHO?

Like Jacob or Michael today, Zechariah
was a very popular name in Bible times.
Your job in this quiz is to sort out
which Zechariah is which.

Answers on next page.

100

What famed evangelist was born to a priest
named Zechariah?

200

At what place of worship was Zechariah, the son
of the high priest Jehoiada, stoned to death for
condemning Judah's idolatry?

300

What violent act ended the reign of the evil King
Zechariah of Israel only six months after he took
power?

400

What structure in Jerusalem did a certain
Zechariah, son of Jonathan, help Nehemiah
dedicate?

500

What type of tree surrounded a man on a red
horse in a vision of the prophet Zechariah?

ZECHARIAH WHO? ANSWERS

100
John the Baptist (Luke 1:57–60)

200
the temple (2 Chronicles 24:17–22)

300
assassination (2 Kings 15:8–10)

400
the wall (Nehemiah 12:27–37)

500
myrtle (Zechariah 1:7–8)

Your Score for This Quiz:
_____Points

Cumulative Score, Z Quizzes:
_____Points

Z INSIDE

Well, what better clue can we give you than that? Every answer in this quiz will include a *Z* somewhere inside.

Answers on next page.

100
What town in Galilee was the boyhood home of Jesus?

200
What word described the crowd's response when Jesus used His authority to drive out evil spirits?

300
What Philistine city's name is still heard in the news today, often with the word "strip"?

400
What "prince of demons" did Pharisees accuse Jesus of using to cast out demons?

500
What town, along with Bethsaida, did not repent when Jesus performed miracles there and thus received a pronouncement of woe?

Z INSIDE ANSWERS

100
Nazareth (Matthew 2:19–23)

200
amazed (Mark 1:23–27)

300
Gaza (2 Kings 18:8)

400
Beelzebul, or Beelzebub (Mark 3:22)

500
Chorazin (Matthew 11:20–21)

Your Score for This Quiz:
_____Points

Cumulative Score, Z Quizzes:
_____Points

ZION

A classic hymn says that "glorious things of thee are spoken, Zion, city of our God." What do you know about this important place?

Answers on next page.

100
What great king of Israel captured the fortress of Zion from mocking Jebusites?

200
What happy musical compositions of Zion did the psalmist remember longingly "by the rivers of Babylon"?

300
What important religious artifact was brought from Zion to the new temple built by Solomon?

400
What kind of stone, according to the apostle Paul, did God lay in Zion?

500
How many of those "redeemed from the earth" stood with the Lamb on Mount Zion in John's Revelation?

ZION ANSWERS

100
David (2 Samuel 5:6–8)

200
songs (Psalm 137:1–3)

300
the ark of the covenant (1 Kings 8:1–5)

400
stumbling (Romans 9:32–33)

500
144,000 (Revelation 14:1–3)

Your Score for This Quiz:
_____ _____Points

Cumulative Score, Z Quizzes:
_____Points

RISK IT!

Zealous People

Well, the four *Z* quizzes are now in the books. . .and it's your final opportunity to *Risk It!* How does a category on "Zealous People" sound? Consider how much of your total score on the *Z* quizzes you want to risk on the one question to follow. If you answer correctly, you add the amount you risked to your total *Z* quiz score. . .if you answer incorrectly, you *subtract* the amount you risked. Are you ready? Mark down the amount you're willing to risk, and we'll unveil the question. . . .

Your Total Score, Z Quizzes:
_____Points

Your Risk It! Amount:
_____ Points

What was the first name of the apostle known as "the zealot" or "Zelotes"?

Answer on next page.

RISK IT! ANSWER

Simon (Luke 6:12–16)

Your Total Score, Z Quizzes:
_____Points

+ or – Your Risk It! Amount:
_____Points

Running Total (A through Z Quizzes):
_____Points

What's a perfect score in *Bible Quiz Show*?
If you answered every question correctly
and successfully risked your total score for
every letter of the alphabet, you'd have
312,000 points! So, how'd you do?

More Bible Fun from
Barbour Publishing

Bible Crossword Challenge

Here are 99 puzzles sure to satisfy
the passionate Bible puzzle fan—all in a
delightful, giftable package! With clues
drawn from the breadth of God's Word,
based on the beloved King James Version,
Bible Crossword Challenge will test and
expand your knowledge of scripture.

Paperback / 978-1-68322-940-7 / $12.99

Find This and More from Barbour
Books at Your Favorite Bookstore
www.barbourbooks.com

BARBOUR
PUBLISHING